THE BIBA YEARS

THE BIBA YEARS

1963–1975

BARBARA HULANICKI AND MARTIN PEL

V&A PUBLISHING

First published by V&A Publishing, 2014
Victoria and Albert Museum
South Kensington
London SW7 2RL
www.vandapublishing.com

Distributed in North America by Harry N. Abrams Inc., New York
© Victoria and Albert Museum, London

The moral right of the authors has been asserted.

Hardback edition
ISBN 978 1 85177 799 0

Library of Congress Control Number 2014932323

10 9 8 7 6 5 4 3 2 1
2018 2017 2016 2015 2014

Every effort has been made to seek permission to reproduce those images
whose copyright does not reside with the V&A, and we are grateful to the
individuals and institutions who have assisted in this task. Any omissions
are entirely unintentional, and the details should be addressed to
V&A Publishing.

Cover: 'Brown Study' featuring Biba Cosmetics, *Nova* (*c*.1969).
Photo: Elisabeth Novick.
Endpapers: Chris Price, *The Great Map of Biba 1964–75*, 2004 (detail).
Originally published in Delisia Howard, Barbara Hulanicki and Chris Price,
In Biba (London 2004).
Frontispiece: Biba catalogue, October 1968 (detail). Photo: Hans Feurer.
Model: Vicki Wise.

New photography by Richard Davis and Tessa Hallmann.
Designer: Lizzie Ballantyne
Copy-editor: Alexandra Stetter
Index: Sue Farr

Printed in China

V&A Publishing

Supporting the world's leading
museum of art and design,
the Victoria and Albert
Museum, London

Contents

Introduction

MARTIN PEL, CURATOR OF COSTUME & TEXTILES

ROYAL PAVILION & MUSEUMS, BRIGHTON & HOVE

For the many millions of customers who stepped through the doors of Biba between 1964 and 1975, the experience proved to be one that few were able, or willing, to forget. Unlike any other fashion label before or since, Biba created a unique atmosphere, which committed the senses to unfamiliar sights, sounds, smells and even tastes.

The Biba mail-order boutique and shops were truly a phenomenon, and it wasn't just the sensory impact of the stores that brought the company such success. The act of wearing, performing in, Biba clothes was an act of transformation – the realization of an idealized self – and would leave an indelible impression on the wearer's psychology. One customer's story perfectly captures this sense of Biba's special status: 'I find it really interesting that I worked in Way In [at Harrods] and owned outfits designed by Ossie Clark, Sheilagh Brown, Sheridan Barnett, Antony Price, Jeff Banks, Betty Jackson and pieces from Electric Fittings, Mr Freedom, Miss Mouse and Hans Metzen. Yet, with a few exceptions, I have only kept Biba.'[1]

Biba was never prescriptive, but offered sartorial freedom and choice, and it brought fashion into the lives of many thousands of women for the first time. The company was not just a retailer of fashionable clothing, however – rather it was the vehicle through which shoppers transformed themselves and their lives. The Biba 'experience' was all about indulgence, so that by the time of the 'Big Biba' store (1973–5), the shop could offer its customers a night's entertainment in the Rainbow Room restaurant or an afternoon tea on the roof garden, and sold everything from Camembert to playing cards. Biba had become the world's first lifestyle label. Barbara Hulanicki, founder

of Biba, maintains that, in the 1960s, the market for young, fashionable clothes at affordable prices was there for the taking. She may be right, but the wider truth is that many thousands of boutiques opened in London, and nationwide, over the 'Swinging Sixties' – yet none of them reached the heights of Biba. Who can remember the boutiques Frivolous (sic) or ARP, to name just two of Biba's contemporaries?

Hulanicki has become a totemic figure for those individuals who wore her clothes in the 1960s and '70s, and Biba has slipped into fashion folklore. Such is the mystique surrounding Biba that it is often thought of by today's younger generation as a high-end ready-to-wear label, or even couture. In fact, Biba was the Topshop of its day, only with added mystery and guile.

I first met Hulanicki at a film screening in 2009, where we discussed the possibility of a retrospective of her work. *Biba and Beyond: Barbara Hulanicki* opened at Brighton Museum in 2012 and went on to be one of the Museum's most successful exhibitions. Like the exhibition, this book sets out to position Hulanicki, and Biba, in the context of their time and their place in fashion history.

In 2010, *The New York Times* acknowledged Hulanicki as the originator of fast fashion, just one of many accolades and awards she has achieved over a lifetime in design. The story of Biba is the story of its creator, the two are indivisible, and the legend and legacy of Biba are Barbara Hulanicki's alone.

Barbara Hulanicki wearing her Aunt Sophie Gassner's gold metal-mesh Chanel jumper, February 1964. Photo: Robert Freson.

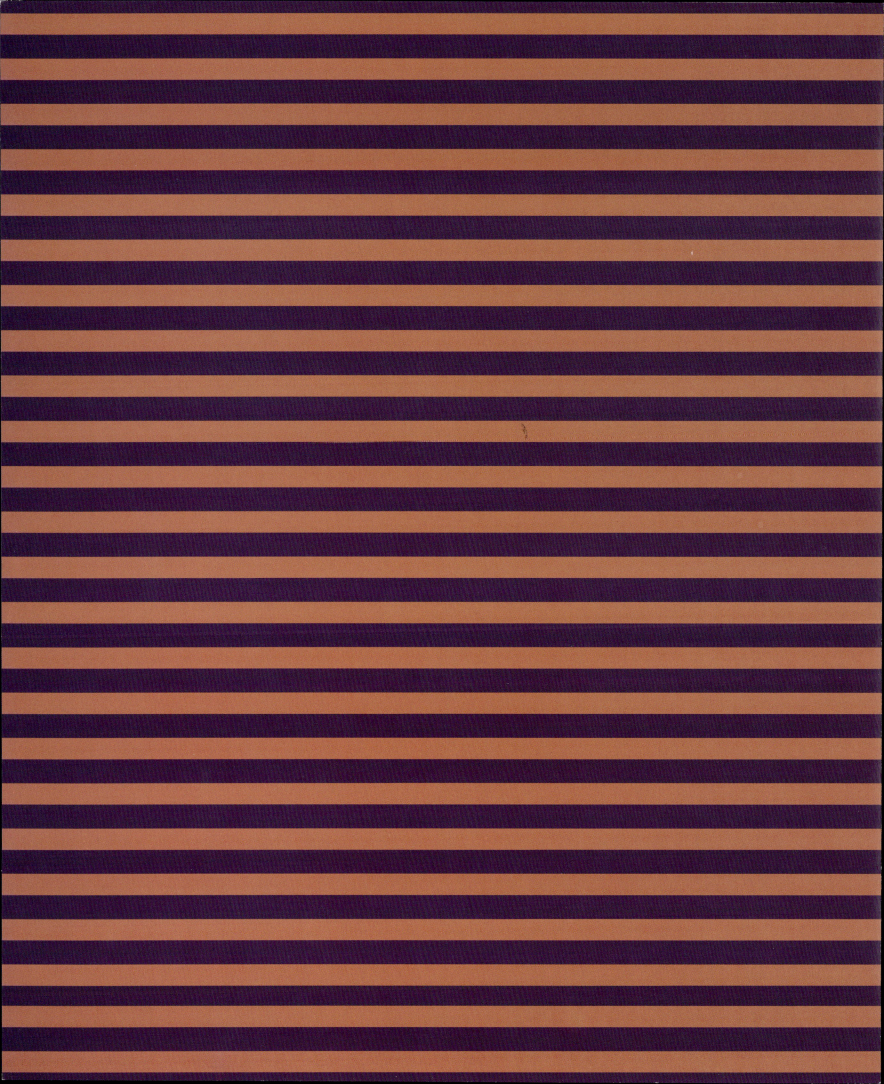

Becoming Biba

1936–1963

'We two kept house, the Past and I'

Thomas Hardy, *The Ghost of the Past*, 1912–13[1]

In the years between the World Wars, London became a focus for the Polish diaspora, as the newly independent Poland suffered political instabilities that culminated in a military coup in 1926. It was here that Witold Hulanicki (below) and Victoria Rein (later Ryan) met in the summer of 1931. Witold had been posted to London three years earlier to serve

Witold Hulanicki in New York, on his way to Los Angeles to captain the Polish Olympic team, 1932

as Poland's consul general; 19-year-old Victoria was boarding at a finishing school in Eastbourne after 'a very turbulent' early life: a childhood spent in Polish convent schools, with an absent father and an overbearing half-sister, Sophie.[2] Nearly 20 years her senior and already married, the Catholic Witold could marry Victoria only after the Vatican had granted the annulment of his previous marriage. The couple settled in Warsaw, where Barbara, their first child, was born on 8 December 1936. Within 18 months, the family had relocated to Jerusalem, where Barbara's two sisters were born: Beatrice in 1938 and Biruta, nicknamed Biba, in 1942.

While living in Jerusalem, the Hulanicki family made infrequent visits to friends and relatives in Warsaw, but on one such occasion they were forced to cut short their holiday. It was the very end of August 1939, and the family abruptly returned to Jerusalem when it became clear that the September Campaign, Germany and the Soviet Union's invasion of Poland, was imminent. The escalation of conflict across Europe and the outbreak of the Second World War effectively isolated the Hulanickis in Jerusalem for the next six years, with Witold leaving his Polish government position and finding work with the British Mandate for Palestine. Many of the relatives they had just visited they would never see again.

In Mandatory Palestine, the family were away from the more extreme deprivations of the war, and life was simple, idyllic and focused on the Hulanicki children.

'Auntie' Sophie Gassner, Barbara and Victoria Hulanicki, c.1937

Barbara Hulanicki remembers the uncomplicated pleasures of her childhood: 'My mother used to draw faces when we were children. We used to sit round watching and then we'd get furious with her if she did a face we didn't like, poor thing. She made us a dolls' house in the cellar with curtains and everything, and we used to sit outside the dolls' house and she used to be drawing faces, little faces.'[3]

Witold's creativity found expression through painting and photography. A semi-professional watercolourist, he produced two illustrated volumes on deep-sea fish, which were published in Jerusalem under the name Witold Biruta. This use of Biruta, the name of one of his two adored sisters and also the name he gave his youngest daughter, indicates the value of family to the Hulanickis. Both Barbara and Beatrice were also given the names of Witold's sisters as middle names. His photography also provides an insight into a close-knit world of family and friends, with innumerable images from the 1930s and '40s showing life in Jerusalem.

From a young age, clothes were more than a mere necessity for Barbara: 'I was a pain to my mother because I didn't want to wear the same clothes as my sisters. I hated these great poufy knickers, which were like a balloon underneath our smock dresses. I was six or seven. I didn't approve. We all had matching clothes, all of us. I rebelled and refused to have these red shoes my sister had, so my poor mother had to find other shoes. It was really tough in Jerusalem because there weren't any shops.'

Victoria Hulanicki saw the deprivations of the war as an opportunity for experimentation and innovation. 'She was always making aftershaves for my father to use, she would make her own witch hazel tonic and she'd make face creams, because you couldn't buy anything,' Barbara recalls. 'Everything you made or sewed or drew. My mother was amazing, she was forever doing things, making things: clothes and stuff for the home.' The luxuries of life were, however, not completely absent, as Witold's privileged

position allowed him the opportunity to travel – and shop – abroad. 'He'd go away a lot to places like Beirut and my mother would say, "Can't you just bring me one thing!?" He'd bring her one thing in 10 colours,' Barbara explains. 'He would go shopping for her and buy these bathing suits – Lebanon was fantastic because they had French clothes, because of the French occupation. They had incredible shoes with platforms, these platforms like Carmen Miranda … I remember he brought her back a two-piece bathing suit, which was knitted. There was a house we used to rent at Lake Tiberias, and she went swimming and couldn't come out because it had grown!'

The young family's settled life came to an abrupt end on 26 February 1948, when Witold Hulanicki was taken from the family home. His body was found the next day,

Witold Hulanicki with his daughters Beatrice (left) and Barbara (right), c.1940

his hands tied and a bullet through his temple. He had been murdered, with the Polish journalist Stefan Arnold, by the paramilitary group Lehi, also known as the Stern Gang, who violently opposed the British presence in Jerusalem and its supporters. The last days of the British Mandate, which ended on 14 May 1948, saw Palestine, and particularly Jerusalem, fall into a state of lawlessness as conflicting factions sought to take control of the region. It is unlikely that the truth of Witold's death will ever be known, but it now seems that he was a casualty of the Cold War, as militants aligned themselves with the anti-British, Soviet-led Communist regime in Poland. 'My father's name was at the top of the list of those to be assassinated by the new Communist Polish Government,' Barbara says.

Witold's death left his wife Victoria inconsolable, effectively making the couple's oldest daughter the emotional head of the family. 'My mother was in a terrible state, terrible. She must have been in such shock and she must have been terrified. Terrified about the future to be left with three young children,' Barbara Hulanicki recalls. 'Thank God the British government was so kind to her, looking after her and getting her on a plane to England with the troops. They were fantastic, because my father had been working for them.' Within a fortnight of the murder, Victoria Hulanicki and the children had relocated to England, eventually settling in Brighton under the apparent benevolence of Victoria's widowed and childless half-sister, Sophie Gassner. A woman of considerable wealth and indeterminate age, Aunt Sophie (also known as 'Auntie') had been left her husband's fortune, made in the cotton industry, on his death five years earlier. Her own halcyon days had been the 1930s, when her life was an endless stream of cocktail parties, couture outfits and planning for the Summer Season. Couturiers Jeanne Lanvin, Jean Patou and Coco Chanel created outfits for her, which she complemented with a collection of furs and jewels. It was an era she decided not to leave, dressing for every daily ritual in her silk crêpe and satin gowns. Aunt Sophie saved the family from an uncertain future but the price was subservience: decisions were made, and paid for, by 'Auntie'. Witold's death was to be *the* defining moment in his daughter Barbara's life; the presence of Aunt Sophie, the influence and motivation throughout her career.

For Barbara Hulanicki, as for many of her generation, cinema was the dominant form of entertainment, and she, like millions of other British teenagers, would watch the latest Hollywood films at the local 'fleapit' – in her case, the Astoria in Gloucester Place, Brighton. Hollywood offered a form of escapism; for Barbara, from the loss of her father and the dominance of her aunt. Submerging herself in Hollywood films starring Deanna Durbin, Greta Garbo, Marlene Dietrich, Grace Kelly and Audrey Hepburn, she imagined an independent life. In a 1966 interview, Hulanicki described the cultural barriers that

also kept her divorced from the realities of her new life in England: 'One of my troubles is the language difficulty. Although I find there's no problem with speaking English … reading something complicated can be more like hard work than pleasure. There are all sorts of things English people take for granted that I don't know, like nursery rhymes and *Winnie the Pooh*. When I read *Alice in Wonderland*, I thought it was gruesome.'[4]

It was at Charmandean, a private school in the nearby town of Worthing, that Barbara found freedom from her home life, and where she met a set of American twins, Marcia and Alicia Bradford. 'We used to have to do art projects and Barbara would always win,' Alicia recalls. 'She had the most amazing colour schemes in her drawings – all these dark plums and purples. Most people just stuck with the boring yellows and blues, but not Barbara, so she'd always win first prize.' Alicia also remembers meeting Aunt Sophie: 'We were really impressed with Barbara.

'Auntie' Sophie Gassner, c.1955

Digby Morton tweed coat and dress modelled by Barbara Goalen for *The Ambassador*, 1950. Photo: John French. V&A: AAD/1979/9

Fashion underwent a radical change in the 1950s, as the haughty demeanour and maternal silhouette epitomized by models such as Barbara Goalen (left) and Fiona Campbell-Walter were rejected in favour of the young and playful. In 1953, British *Vogue* launched a regular feature, 'Young Idea', showcasing clothes for girls and young women aged between 17 and 25 and, two years later, in November 1955, Mary Quant opened her boutique Bazaar on the King's Road in Chelsea. The 'Youthquake' of the 1960s (the term was coined in 1965 by Diana Vreeland, then editor-in-chief of American *Vogue*) was informed by the simple, unstructured designs of Quant: 'I just knew that I wanted to concentrate on finding the right clothes for the young to wear,' Quant recalls.[6] But while Quant's clothes were youthful, they were priced for wealthy Chelsea Girls – for middle-class women with a youthful attitude and figure, aged between 20 and 40 – not your average girl in the street.

Janey Ironside, former dressmaker to London's elite, was appointed as a professor of fashion at the Royal College of Art (RCA) in 1956, and this move would also prove to be nothing short of 'revolutionary'.[7] Ironside's aim was to 'promote an internationally accepted new English look', prompting her to open the RCA to students with a wealth of talent, rather than simply a privileged background.[8] In doing so, Ironside produced a whole slew of successful British designers, including James Wedge, Zandra Rhodes, Marion Foale and Sally Tuffin, David Sassoon and, later, Ossie Clark, Bill Gibb and Antony Price.

In the 1950s, the acquisition of affordable yet fashionable clothing became a preoccupation for Barbara Hulanicki, as it was for many girls of her generation. Garments made up from paper patterns provided one option, although they were not always the success Hulanicki hoped for. 'My mother was always sewing and I would start sewing things and then I'd get bored,' she says. 'My mother couldn't stand to see these half-made things so she would have to finish them, and I was forever saying, "No Mama, make it tighter!"'

Aunt Sophie was keen for her niece to take a place at university but Barbara, against her aunt's wishes, attended Brighton College of Art. It was here that Hulanicki began to learn the skills and make the acquaintances that would influence her choices in both her life and her career. While at art school she met and became engaged to

Her auntie had a chinchilla coat, which was something we'd never seen before. It was so sophisticated.'[5] The twins made an indelible impression and their style was a lasting influence on Barbara, opening her eyes to American fashion aimed at the new, and as yet untapped, teenage market: 'They were my heroes. They had these wonderful clothes from America. Every new term they would have these gorgeous dresses; there would be one in pink and the other one in blue, these fantastic Fifties dresses. They had these modern clothes, modern colours. And we had terrible uniforms.'

Peter Dingemans, an officer in the navy. The relationship did not last, with Hulanicki breaking off the engagement, unsure whether the life of a serviceman's wife was for her, but she remained great friends with the family, especially Peter's two sisters, Jennie and Jo. Jennie Dingemans recalls a friend's twenty-first birthday party: 'I've got very vivid memories of Barbara wearing an ice-blue gown. She looked terrific and it was so elegant and so unusual for that time because it was her aunt's.'[9] Jo Dingemans, who was eight years old at the time, also remembers the future designer: 'Barbara would drag me into our ping-pong room and say, "Put this hat on and stand over there", and she'd sketch. Whatever you looked like, the drawings were beautiful – great big eyes.'[10] Jennie adds, 'One was mesmerized by her drawings, which she did of these models with great big eyes, pictures that we'd never seen before.'[11] Pauline Ratty, who taught Hulanicki at Brighton College of Art, also remembers the young Barbara:

'She'd got this flair, she had a definite Fifties style about her, but she didn't create traditional design, very far from it. She did these girls with these sweet little faces and navy blue eyelids, or bright green eyelids and short skirts that shot out at the side ... lovely colours, lovely things.'[12]

A visiting lecturer from the RCA cajoled, intimidated and pushed Barbara Hulanicki into her first career. Joanne Brogden, assistant to Janey Ironside and later herself professor of fashion at the RCA, taught drawing and illustration at Brighton. Hulanicki says that when, in 1956, she passed her second-year exam with a smock dress with pocket flaps but no pockets, Brogden exclaimed, 'I don't believe you passed, I can't believe it. You're much better at drawing, go and draw.'

Below, left: Barbara Hulanicki, beachwear design for a competition held by the *Evening Standard*, mixed media, 1955

Below, right: 'The smile of success', *Evening Standard*, c.1955

Brogden's comments were probably influenced by a recent success of Hulanicki's. The *Evening Standard* had run a fashion contest the year before, with a panel of four judges including Norman Hartnell – couturier to the Queen, and to Aunt Sophie. Under the 'guidance' of her aunt, Hulanicki had submitted a design for a fussy day dress. Inspired to design her own garment, she also secretly entered an Italian-style beach outfit in candy-striped cotton with a white Eton collar (previous page). In her illustration for the design, she imagined Audrey Hepburn in *Sabrina Fair* (1954) wearing the outfit. Hulanicki went on to win the beachwear section of the competition, as well as the displeasure of Auntie: 'There was a stony silence while she regained her composure.'[13]

Hulanicki's success in the beachwear competition was to be her first demonstrable break from Aunt Sophie's control, and the prize for winning the competition only contributed to the waning of Auntie's influence. Hartnell's couture house made up each of the winning designs and Hulanicki, accompanied by her aunt, visited his Bruton Street salon in London's Mayfair, to be presented with her outfit: 'I went up to his grand showroom with Auntie and it was my first introduction to the couture world and he'd coutured [sic] it! I was in shock.' In the hands of the couturier, her soft cotton outfit became a silk taffeta confection more suited

Barbara Hulanicki, assorted fashion illustrations commissioned by *Vogue*, 1964

to a cocktail party than a beach holiday. 'They wouldn't have used cotton,' she explains, 'cotton was really downmarket.' Winning the competition was confirmation of Hulanicki's ability as a designer, and the success and public recognition gave her confidence and a thirst for even greater successes. The competition's official prize may have been a disappointment but the effect of this episode was revelatory, and Barbara Hulanicki left art college before completing her course to forge a career of her own.

With an effortless dedication to drawing that comes from natural aptitude, Hulanicki sought work in the world of illustration. She sent a 'cheeky letter' to a London advertising agency, Helen Jardine Artists: 'I had an interview and was given a job immediately, making tea! I did this for a couple of months and then they sent me out to some crummy little agent, these funny little advertising agencies that did corsets, underwear and girdles. That was a huge business and I was freelance drawing for a long time.' With permanent employment and a good wage, Hulanicki left Brighton in 1957 and moved to London, sharing a flat on Douro Place in Kensington with five other girls. 'I had to move out in the end, there was a constant party going on there,' she recalls. While based at Helen Jardine Artists, she also began working for J. Walter Thompson, one of the world's leading advertising agencies, where she would meet Willie Landels, the influential art director of *Queen* magazine, and, later, the art and fashion editors of the glossy fashion press – individuals who would have a significant impact on Hulanicki and her career.

The late 1950s also brought Barbara Hulanicki together, for the first time, with Stephen Fitz-Simon (above right), the person who would change the direction of her life, and who would work with her to change the course of British fashion. Known by his family and friends as Fitz, Fitz-Simon was born in Surbiton, Surrey, in 1937 and attended Beaumont College, the prestigious public school in Berkshire. A champion runner as a schoolboy, he had competed against the future Olympic athlete Christopher Chataway. Fitz-Simon was working as an accounts executive in an advertising agency when he met Hulanicki at a party – he was the worse for wear and she unimpressed. It wasn't until early 1961 that they were to meet again, but by November of that year, they were married and living on Kensington's Cromwell Road.

Stephen Fitz-Simon on National Service, England, c.1955

Married life gave Hulanicki the emotional support she needed to extend her career. Freelancing as an illustrator for the print media, she worked for editors and journalists such as Felicity Green (fashion editor of the *Daily Mirror*), Barbara Griggs (fashion editor of the *Evening Standard*), Liz Dickson (fashion editor of *Queen*), Max Maxwell (art director of *Vogue*) and Annie Trehearne (fashion editor of *Queen*). She covered the bi-annual couture shows in Paris, with designers such as Dior, Balenciaga and Balmain unveiling their new designs, their new silhouettes – dictating the style of dress that women, young and old, would soon be wearing the world over. 'I spent about three years going to all the shows in Paris doing illustration. They went on for hours and hours, always the same old thing,' Hulanicki recalls. 'All the models were skin and bone and really snooty, apart from one, Christine Tidmarsh.

She was always doing Dior and she'd come bounding down, and everybody would be, like, "thank God", because then you'd wake up.'

This freelance work brought economic rewards but also uncertainty: 'I would get the commission before I went but you still had to pay your travel and hotel.' Hulanicki would attend each show but her work would not begin until the next day, when the journalist responsible for the fashion story had chosen which outfit to include. 'And then it was a private thing between the model and me. I would go to the couture house and the model would come out and stand there huffing and puffing,' she explains. 'All they wanted was the cash, because I had to pay them cash at the end, so I had to be really fast. It was amazing really because it trains your visual memory; it's got to go in there. It was like learning lines.'

It was at one such couture show that Hulanicki saw her idol, Audrey Hepburn, in the flesh – the actress was attending a Givenchy show in preparation for the film *Paris When It Sizzles* (1964) – but the encounter proved to be a disappointment. Rather than the elfin figure Hulanicki had seen projected on screen, Hepburn had an athletic build thanks to her erstwhile career as a ballerina. Her clothes, rather than the doll-like creations of Hulanicki's imagining, were larger and sturdier and clearly made with purpose: 'I almost wish I'd never seen her, it broke the celluloid magic.'

Hulanicki's uninspiring first experience of couture at Hartnell's salon in 1955 was only reinforced by her work at the Paris couture shows: 'There was nothing which made your heart go pitter-patter. All I wanted were clothes that didn't look like that, because that was my mother and my aunt, that's how they dressed. They were all sort of cocktail clothes.' An incident that occurred while she

Right: 'Balenciaga & Givenchy' with illustrations by Barbara Hulanicki, *Tatler* (20 March 1963)

Overleaf (clockwise from top-left): Barbara Hulanicki, 'Greta Garbo' sketch, work on paper, c.1958; 'Biba head' drawing, work on paper, c.1959; 'Biba body' drawing, work on paper, c.1959; 'Audrey Hepburn' girl in ballet-style underwear, sketch for an advertisement, mixed media, c.1963

Overleaf, right: Barbara Hulanicki, 'Audrey Hepburn' sketch, work on paper, c.1961

High on the list of things worth waiting for comes the spring line from the two most elegant arbiters of fashion in Paris. Barbara Hulanicki illustrates

BALENCIAGA & GIVENCHY

International set suit: in supple, chunky, emerald and beige flecked tweed with slender skirt, jacket finished with a rouleau tie at the waist, a roll collar and cork buttons. Cloche in navy para straw. **BALENCIAGA**

Dip into summer colour for instant elegance: primrose tweed coat with curved collar and set shoulders, caught above the waist with one button. Worn with a paler yellow wool jersey sleeveless shift and blue toque. Shifty note: two curved pockets, roll collar and waist slashed with a leather rouleau, gilt and pearl pin at the neck. **GIVENCHY**

was working for John Fairchild at *Women's Wear Daily* in London would prove pivotal. 'I was drawing the collections of couturiers like Michael, Hardy Amies and Norman Hartnell,' Hulanicki recalls, 'and I will never forget John Fairchild, Michael and Hardy Amies giving me such a lecture because I didn't get the shape right of Michael's concave front.' Her inclination to 'correct' the models' habit of projecting their shoulders and hips slightly forward to create a fashionable, concave look had brought disapproval from the fashion establishment, but it would prove salutary: 'You always felt you were learning a lot,

Opposite: Barbara Hulanicki working on an illustration, 1964

Below: Barbara Hulanicki's diary showing her work schedule for the Paris fashion shows, 25 September to 1 October 1961

but the more you saw, the more you were convinced that you were right.'

Fitz-Simon was once again instrumental in influencing a career change. 'Without him I would never have done the designing,' Hulanicki explains. 'Fitz was really on the ball. He worked in advertising and he could see that photography was coming in. He said to me, "You've got to stop doing [fashion illustration], it's going to come to an end. You've got to get back into design."' The new role came naturally to Hulanicki, her career as a fashion illustrator unwittingly making her an instinctive designer. As a freelance fashion illustrator, she had realized that bold lines were better suited to printing and therefore more saleable than impressionistic representations of a garment. Strong silhouettes rather than surface detail

became characteristic of her aesthetic and she carried this style through into her design work. The need to make her illustrations as aesthetically appealing as possible also led Hulanicki to 'adjust' what she considered to be the less attractive aspects of a garment's design.

Garment production was a different world altogether, one unknown to both Hulanicki and Fitz-Simon. 'You can't just design dresses and that's it, there's got to be the whole production side, which Fitz learnt. He went and got to know all the manufacturers and they all loved him,' she recalls. 'There was Mr Savva – he was wonderful, a Greek Cypriot. He got on with Fitz really well and they would go Greek dancing after hours and throw plates, as there was a big social scene. I don't know how we found him, he just fell into our life; everybody fell into our lives.'

The summer of 1963 saw Hulanicki and Fitz-Simon launch a fashion mail-order company. Mail order grew at an unprecedented rate during the 1960s, outstripping all other forms of retailing and offering every available type of consumer goods. Companies such as Freemans, Littlewoods and Grattan offered easy shopping on credit, often with weekly payment instalments, to working-class consumers. For a small company, mail order was also the most economical way to operate: with only the orders already paid for then manufactured, they could avoid having to invest in a ready-made supply of stock. The new business would advertise itself as a boutique. 'I didn't want my own name associated with it,' Hulanicki explains. 'I wanted people to focus on the concept of our company – inexpensive fashion for everyone – rather than a personality. Fitz and I thought of a few names but they all brought to mind the wrong ideas. We decided on Biba, my little sister's nickname. It was feminine and unusual, a name people could bring their own ideas to. We tried it out on friends and one friend's boyfriend, who happened to be a Russian prince, said, "Oh dear, the name is terrible, it's a char lady's daughter's name", and I was like, Hooray!'

The first advert for Biba's Postal Boutique appeared in the *Daily Express* in early June 1963. It featured a design for a simple drawstring maxi skirt in brushed cotton, available in four colours: brown, mustard, black and red (opposite). The ankle-length, Edwardian-style skirt was in contrast to the short shift dresses produced by young London designers that year, such as Foale & Tuffin (graduates of the RCA), and Roger Nelson, its style more in keeping with the 'Miss Jean Brodie' look of fashion manufacturer Susan Small from a year or so earlier.

Above: Logo for Biba's Postal Boutique designed by John McConnell, 1964

Left: Barbara Hulanicki, working drawing of black and polka-dot dresses, mixed media, 1964

Opposite: Barbara Hulanicki, working drawing of the first Biba's Postal Boutique skirt, mixed media, 1963

The maxi skirt represents Hulanicki's first tentative step into the world of design rather than a statement of design intent and, with its uncomplicated construction, it allowed the manufacturing process to be kept simple. Hulanicki's old tutor Joanne Brogden had provided students to make the first sample and to fulfil the orders, and Fitz-Simon sourced a small textile producer. With a few hundred orders, their first foray into the fashion business was a qualified success. The following two advertisements were not so well received and, with limited orders, it appeared the venture was going to end before it had begun. Undeterred, however, Hulanicki continued to design and Fitz-Simon to oversee production and promotion.

Over the coming months, the orders for Biba's Postal Boutique would fluctuate from a few hundred to a few dozen, giving Hulanicki an opportunity to gain a better understanding of the public's taste for recognizably youth-oriented, individual clothing and Fitz-Simon a chance to iron out production problems. Some designs received no orders at all – for example, a child's denim dress and the 'wigchief', a headscarf with a fringe of hair attached (an idea Hulanicki resurrected, with huge success, five years later). The year 1963 ended with both of them still in their full-time jobs and Biba's Postal Boutique as a hobby with potential.

Below: Barbara Hulanicki, working drawings for children's outfits, mixed media, c.1964

Opposite: Girl's shift dress, advertisement for Biba's Postal Boutique, *Evening Standard*, 31 March 1964

'We started off with just really simple shapes, little smocks and shifts, as it kept the manufacturing headaches away when we were starting.'[†]

87 Abingdon Road

1964–1966

'There should be a plaque on 87 Abingdon Road. It transformed the way the ordinary girl in the street dressed ... it was a tiny corner shop, an old chemist's in a quiet residential street. But before long, Biba was Mecca to everyone from shop girls to debs ... Not only did the clothes look amazing, you could afford to buy something every week.'

Twiggy Lawson, *Twiggy in Black and White*, 1997[1]

After the coldest Easter in 80 years, the summer of 1964 was unusually hot, with almost uninterrupted sun and blue skies until October. It was to be a year of change. That autumn saw a general election: the old-guard Conservative government pitted against the vanguard of Labour's New Britain – 'forged in the white heat of [scientific] revolution' and poised to capitalize on the growing confidence of British industry.[2]

The Conservatives, who had been in power for the past 13 years, had a new party leader – Sir Alec Douglas-Home, Britain's last Prime Minister to be a member of the House of Lords. Labour also had a new leader: the grammar-school-educated Harold Wilson, who represented change and egalitarianism. Wilson won the day, but only by the narrowest of margins (an overall majority of four seats), forcing him to call another general election in 1966. Britain's vote for change was on probation.

In fashion, the French couturier André Courrèges presented his controversial and groundbreaking *Space Age* collection in the spring of 1964. With more than a nod to young London designers and fashions, this collection's

Paulene Stone modelling Hulanicki's pink gingham dress, back view, Daily Mirror, May 1964. Photo: John French.

pared-down aesthetic – simple shapes in stark white, exposing models' midriffs and legs – prompted the bible of the fashion industry, *Women's Wear Daily*, to dub Courrèges the 'Le Corbusier of fashion'.[3] Resolutely modern, the collection was a deliberate attempt to break away from the elaborate style of traditional French couture but, at £230 for a coat, Courrèges himself was to admit, 'it would be more up to date to have low prices. I will try and find a way.'[4]

In 1964, everything fell into place for Biba's Postal Boutique. The company was barely a year old and its owners had been on a steep learning curve, with notable successes and numerous failures. One newspaper feature would bring together all of those lessons learnt, with the addition of two crucial elements: celebrity and availability.

Felicity Green, the fashion editor of the *Daily Mirror*, had commissioned Barbara Hulanicki to produce illustrations for her newspaper column since the early 1960s. 'This apparition walked through the door, it was one of her drawings absolutely brought to life,' she says of her first encounter with Hulanicki. 'She had exactly the right long blonde hair, uninterrupted by curls, and the clothes she wore were the ones in the illustrations. She was a style emblem right from that moment, and I was so taken with her appearance that I wanted to capture it, because it was so different to what everybody else was doing. To dress like that and do drawings like that and be so eloquent ... If ever I had faith in somebody's future ... [as] a journalist you have a nose, whether it's writing, photography – you have an instinct and it's very, very immediate.'[5]

In the spring of 1964, Green's double-page article, entitled 'Four girls prove that beauty and business ideas can go together', featured Letizia Adam, a handbag designer; Sally Simpson, a couturier; Marie Lise Boyle, the owner of a newly opened hair salon; and Barbara Hulanicki, 'a dress manufacturer as well as a fashion artist' (opposite).[6] Readers were offered the opportunity to buy a gingham shift dress designed by Hulanicki: 'If you're in the market for something cool and shifty ... If you think gingham is an "in" fabric ... if you feel

twenty-five bob isn't a fashion fortune – and it isn't ... This is your dress, with its figure skimming lines, softly rolling neckline and keyhole back.'[7] Green wanted to keep the price as low as possible and, after some negotiation with Hulanicki, the price of 25 shillings was agreed, which was, Barbara concedes, 'cheap, even in those days'.

That summer saw fashion journalist Mary Borgan advise in the *Sunday Telegraph*, 'There is nothing like cotton for really hot weather', a message that became a fashion leitmotif for the season, as a slew of light cotton dresses hit the market.[8] The Dollyrockers label, designed by Samuel Sherman (known as Sambo) and sold in high-street shops, offered a denim high-waisted dress with broderie anglaise detail for 75s and, for the more monied shopper, Foale & Tuffin had, at nine-and-a-half guineas, a 'high-waisted shift in cool, checked cotton in easy and unconstricting [sic] shape for hot weather'.[9]

Hulanicki's simple shift dress in sugar-pink gingham, with matching headscarf and available by mail order, was the right dress at the right moment and, at 25s, was accessible to almost anybody. Fitz-Simon calculated that, with an average weekly wage of £9, a girl would spend £3 on rent, £3 on food and £3 on clothes.[10]

The headscarf, inspired by a recent photograph of Brigitte Bardot, 'the queen of gingham', gave the outfit an informal glamour.[11] Green's article was also accompanied by a photograph of model Paulene Stone (whom Hulanicki had been in awe of when she saw her wafting around their shared home town of Brighton in the 1950s), taken by established society photographer John French. Characterized by low contrast and the use of natural light, French's work was, according to Barbara Griggs, the fashion editor of the *Evening Standard*, 'made for newspaper print'.[12]

Within a few days of the article's publication on 1 May 1964, 500 orders had been received. By the end of the week it was a few thousand, a figure that would multiply over the coming weeks. Initial elation soon turned to frustration as the response began to overwhelm Hulanicki

Above: Revised logo for Biba's Postal Boutique designed by John McConnell, 1964

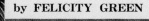

by FELICITY GREEN

DAILY MIRROR, Friday, May 1, 1964   PAGE 17

Four girls prove that beauty and business ideas can go together

THIS IS LETIZIA

SHE DESIGNS AND IMPORTS HANDBAGS.

Letizia, married to film designer Ken Adam—Dr. Strangelove, Dr. No—found friends drooling over the bags she had made to her own design in Italy, her homeland.

So if everyone liked them and wanted them, why didn't she organise it so they could have them? She lined up the workmen in Rome and Florence, provided them with the necessary sketches, and suddenly she was in the handbag business.

Now imports them in quantity and has them on sale in THE most exclusive West End shops. Expensive—from 22 to 120 gns. "But chicissimo," says Letizia, "and just what women want."

THIS IS SALLY

SOON SHE'LL HAVE HER OWN COUTURE BUSINESS.

Some time early next month ex-model Sally Simpson, who confesses to being bored rigid after two years before the camera, opens up her own couture business, "Vanilla."

Her task—designing and making to measure clothes for fashion-conscious clients with an eye for the exclusive and a bank balance that doesn't balk at a starting price of £30.

The styles will be young and pretty and designed by Sally and her partner.

Why "Vanilla"? "Everyone asks that," says Sally, "so it obviously makes an impression."

THIS IS MARIE LISE

SHE'S OPENING A BOUTIQUE FOR "WIGS AND PRETTY THINGS."

On Monday of next week the ground floor of one of London's newest and most glamorous hairdressing establishments—it's five floors, so you can't call it a salon—will be taken over by Marie Lise.

What will be on sale? Shoes, scarves, belts, jewellery and handbags, all designed by the French-born boss herself. Also hair pieces designed in collaboration with her husband, wigmaker Simon Boyle.

"I think people want pretty, individual things—and not too expensive, either," says Marie Lise. "The hair pieces, for instance, will start at 4 gns."

THIS IS BARBARA

NOW SHE'S A DRESS MANUFACTURER AS WELL AS A FASHION ARTIST.

One of the most successful fashion artists in the business, Barbara went to a party in a long skirt she had made herself. A fashion editor saw it, adored it, and wanted a similar one for her readers. So Barbara got a friend in the cheaper end of the rag-trade to make it up in quantities at a next-to-nothing price.

Hundreds of people sent for it. Now she designs specially for newspapers and magazines on a mailorder only basis. On the right a "Barbara" summer shift designed exclusively for Daily Mirror readers. For more about this, read on. . . .

.. and this is one of her designs. Interested? It can be yours for 25s including the kerchief

✳ If you're in the market for something cool and shifty . . .
If you think gingham is an "in" fabric . . .
If you like the idea of the headscarf to match . . .
If you feel twenty-five bob isn't a fashion fortune—and it isn't . . .
This is your dress, with its figure-skimming lines, softly rolling neckline and keyhole back.
It has been designed and made specially for the Daily Mirror by Barbara Hulanicki.
If you would like one, send 25s., plus 1s. 6d. for postage and packing, to Biba's Postal Boutique, 35, Oxford-street, London, W.1.
In pink gingham. Sizes: 10, 12, 14.

and Fitz-Simon. They were forced to call in family and friends to deal with the volume of mail. A more serious problem arose with the need to manufacture the outfit in large quantities. Their 400-yard supply of gingham wasn't enough to fulfill even the first day's orders and it looked as if the business would stumble at its first major success. Stephen Fitz-Simon and Humphrey Rowlands, Victoria Hulanicki's partner, made enquiries nationwide before finding a supply of pink gingham with the textile manufacturer Burgess Ledward. Established in the nineteenth century, Burgess Ledward rescued the fledgling company and went on to become a reliable source and treasure trove of fabrics for Hulanicki.

Eventual orders of the dress numbered over 17,000 and its success provided a business model for the fledgling company.[13] Over the summer of 1964, Hulanicki produced a number of designs that were similar in fabric and style, but orders never went beyond a few hundred. A significant factor in the success of the pink gingham dress was its price: the deal Hulanicki had struck with Felicity Green, much to Fitz-Simon's initial consternation, left them with only a small profit but with orders so high that they

Felicity Green, 'Four girls prove that beauty and business ideas can go together', with photograph by John French of Paulene Stone modelling the pink gingham dress, *Daily Mirror*, 1 May 1964

generated significant cash flow. This model would become a guiding principle for Fitz-Simon, who happily informed the interior designer Julie Hodgess some years later: 'Remember Julie, pennies make pounds.'[14] The gingham dress's associations with celebrity and glamour – with Brigitte Bardot, Paulene Stone and John French – gave

Above, left: Barbara Hulanicki, illustration of pink and blue shift dresses, mixed media, c.1964

Above, right: 'Sit back and make it easy', advertisement for Biba's Postal Boutique with illustration by Barbara Hulanicki, *Daily Express*, 22 June 1964

an already intrinsically desirable garment added kudos and, with promotion through a national newspaper, it had an instant and broad market. These lessons became, subconsciously, the Biba philosophy. Work roles at the company fell naturally into place, with Fitz-Simon looking after business and Hulanicki overseeing creative output. 'I was always getting bored and on to the next thing,' she explains. 'I was always tomorrow and Fitz was today.'

As early as November 1957, an article published in the American magazine *Cosmopolitan* asked 'Are Teenagers Taking Over?'[15] British teenagers in the late 1950s and early '60s had considerable spending power, estimated to be worth £800 million in 1960, with the effect that sales of 45 rpm single records, for example, increased from four

million units in 1955 to 61 million in 1963.[16] Manufacturers of fashionable clothing had, through arrogance and lack of understanding, failed to capitalize on this lucrative new market: Victor Edelstein, who would join Biba as a pattern cutter in 1967, remembers attending job interviews in the early 1960s at companies that defensively declared, 'We don't have anything like that Mary Quant here.'[17]

This new market was unfamiliar territory for established manufacturers and adjustment came slowly, if at all: 'Post-war British society has little experience in providing for prosperous working-class teenagers ... [and they] more than any other section of the community are looking for goods and services which are highly charged emotionally. To appreciate this is ... something which is not easy for a middle-aged industrialist whose comparable enthusiasms and struggles took place in a world that died 30 or 40 years ago.'[18] If the artist Richard Hamilton's credo for Pop art – that it was 'Popular (designed for a mass audience), Transient (short-term solution), Expendable (easily forgotten), Low-cost, Mass-produced, Young (aimed at Youth), Witty, Sexy, Gimmicky, Glamourous [sic], Big Business'– accurately reflected the ethos of the age, then the newly named Biba (abbreviated from Biba's Postal Boutique) was to be its perfect expression, and representative of the democratic ideals of the 1960s.[19]

In between the 'coldest Easter' and the formation of Britain's new Labour government, Hulanicki and Fitz-Simon had opened a small shop on Kensington's Abingdon Road (opposite and overleaf). The impetus was a sale Hulanicki had held in their Cromwell Road flat. The mail-order business had left them with a number of returned garments, which were taking up space in their home and at the manufacturers' premises. The couple promoted the sale to contacts in Hulanicki's personal address book and by word-of-mouth, a form of advertising that would take Biba through its first significant years of success. With the left-over stock judiciously displayed across every available surface in the flat – chairs, tables and even walls – and with the Beatles playing at full volume on the record player, the clothes sold out in a matter of hours, leaving Hulanicki with £500 in an old shoebox and an idea in her head. As with the success of the gingham dress, the sale proved unequivocally that Britain's – or at least London's – teenage girls and young working women were desperate for well-designed clothes at affordable prices, which could be worn *today*. 'Investment' clothes were for the make-do-and-mend generation or the monied elite. 'The market was instant for that age group,' Hulanicki recalls, 'they wanted it there and then. They didn't want to wait, as they didn't look to the future in any way. We always sold everything right on the nose, we never sold [clothes] too early or too late [in the season] the way they do now.'

Biba at 87 Abingdon Road opened its doors for the first time on 5 September 1964 and, without advertising or even a sign above the door, its stock sold out on the first day. The only voice of dissent had come from Barbara Hulanicki's personal accountant, who considered the opening of a shop to be a costly extravagance and an unwise move. For Hulanicki and Fitz-Simon, there was never any doubt that the shop would succeed: 'When you're in your twenties nothing is a gamble. You're just so optimistic about everything.'

The September opening was a sound commercial decision and common to three of the five Biba shops that the couple went on to open. Fitz-Simon was aware that September was one of the best months of the year for business. 'We always opened in September because that's when you can take a lot of money because of coats,' Hulanicki explains. 'The actual price of a coat is equal to four dresses.'

Biba's success would spawn a thousand imitators in 'boutique culture' over the next few years. The booming British economy meant that household goods such as televisions, washing machines and refrigerators were within reach of millions of families across Britain in the 1950s. Fashion also became a mass commodity, reflecting Britain's growing wealth in the post-war years, and the newly launched Sunday colour supplements (*The Sunday Times* magazine first appeared in 1962, with the *Observer* and the *Telegraph* magazines following in 1964) mirrored and fuelled Britain's consumer society. Fashion ostensibly offered another level of desirable consumer goods, but clothing's inherent relationship with the body was also to provide the magazines with provocative and occasionally

Below: Exterior of Biba, 87 Abingdon Road, London, c.1964

Overleaf: Biba 'Op art' dress modelled outside Biba, 87 Abingdon Road, London, c.1965

'The market was instant
for that age group,
they wanted it there and then.
They didn't want to wait,
as they didn't look to the future
in any way.'

titillating images to fill their pages. These 'free' magazines brought fashion, previously the preserve of the wealthy or initiated, into every home in the country, and fashion became an increasingly valuable indicator of status.

A key element in the growing success of Biba was Hulanicki's decision to employ an in-house pattern cutter in the summer of 1964. Ann Behr, who had been a contemporary of Hulanicki's at Brighton Art School, studying Fine Art, joined the company to translate Biba designs, initially into samples and then into patterns ready for production. Since the beginning of Biba's Postal Boutique, all of the patterns had been produced by the fashion students at the Royal College of Art (RCA),

but in Behr, Hulanicki found a kindred spirit, someone who instinctively understood the look she was trying to achieve. One of the first patterns Behr worked on was for Biba's first trouser suit. During the 1950s, the idea of trousers as informal womenswear had gained ground and acceptability, in the guise of Capri pants, jeans and drainpipe trousers. Courrèges's 1964 collection brought the mini-skirt and the trouser suit for women into the world of couture. This was merely one expression of the general trend in dressing young, modern women; Nina Ricci presented her women's trouser suit in Paris the same year, as did young London-based designers who were dressing the girl on the street, though acceptance of the trouser suit was not immediate. 'When [television presenter] Cathy McGowan first wore a trouser suit to the Savoy [Hotel] she was thrown out,' Hulanicki recalls. 'It was all over the front page because she wore trousers. Pathetic, isn't it? It was just frumpy old people, the same people that complain about gays.' *She* magazine, which had a more conservative readership, picked out Biba's first trouser suit in October 1964 as 'an outstanding value-for-glamour bargain obtainable throughout the whole country', although it did reassure its readers that the suit had 'a slim skirt for the timid' (opposite).[20]

Biba's pinstripe trouser suit, which sold for 7gns (jacket at 4gns, trousers 3gns), was to be the first notable success for the new Biba boutique and featured in one of the earliest newspaper articles on the newly opened shop. Barbara Griggs, the fashion editor of the *Evening Standard*, had, like Felicity Green at the *Daily Mirror*, featured Hulanicki's illustrations in her fashion pages for a number of years and she was keen to support the new boutique. 'Barbara did gorgeous drawings, she was very obviously very, very gifted,' Griggs recalls. 'I wasn't surprised when she got going as a designer. The way she drew was original and the clothes looked like clothes for somebody here and now.'[21] As well as being an endorsement for the new venture, Griggs's article, entitled 'Let me be the first to tell you …' (left), also represented

Left: Barbara Griggs, 'Let me be the first to tell you...', *Evening Standard*, 26 October 1964

Opposite: 'National Prize' featuring Biba trouser suit, *She* (October 1964). Photo: David Steen.

DAVID STEEN

NATIONAL PRIZE

Al Capone will be turning in his grave. He liked his women in satin and ostrich feathers. This trouser suit with a gangster touch would be devastating at the office, delicious at the weekend, has a slim skirt for the timid.
Especially designed for **SHE** by Biba's Postal Boutique, 10 Blenheim Street, London, W.1.
Jacket **4 gns.** Trousers **3 gns.** Skirt (not shown) **2 gns.** Slouch hat **1 gn.**
And for quick-getaway girls, a Moulton bicycle, De luxe of course, for **£31/19/6.**

Shops and Sizes page 130

Shoes by Russell & Bromley

a recognition that fashion was undergoing radical changes. It featured a large picture of pattern cutter Ann Behr in the pinstripe trouser suit and reflected the expanding social roles of women in 1960s Britain, as they became businesswomen and entrepreneurs.

By 1966 the *Daily Mail* was able to report that 'Girls will be Boys', declaring that 'Like it or not – and many men don't – trouser suits for girls are here to stay.'[22] In a feature presenting a selection of the best trouser suits, the first in line was a brown-and-cream jersey suit by Biba, priced at 7gns (the same price as the pinstripe suit of 18 months earlier). Alongside Biba's offering were a white wool suit by Foale & Tuffin at 20gns, Gerald McCann's navy wool trouser suit at 18-and-a-half gns, and Bourne & Hollingsworth's red-and-white striped suit (jacket seven-and-a-half gns, trousers 89s 6d). Competing equally in style with the other labels, the Biba trouser suit outstripped them all in price.

Julie Christie wore the trouser suit in the 1965 film *Darling*, in the first instance of Biba on film (below).

Its inclusion was a thrill for both Hulanicki and Fitz-Simon, but the pinstripe suit also held more personal memories for Barbara. 'The last time I saw my father, the morning he said goodbye to me before he was murdered, he was wearing a brown pinstripe suit,' she recalls. Nostalgia and Biba were to become synonymous, and recapturing the past Hulanicki's aesthetic signature. In a photograph accompanying Griggs's article, Hulanicki is shown standing next to bentwood hatstands, heavy with black, Victorian-style day dresses with white lace collars and cuffs

Victoriana and the style of the interwar years were yet to influence mainstream fashion, only coming to the fore in the late 1960s, but were part of the Biba look from the beginning. Alongside the more contemporary minidresses and trouser suits sold in Biba, there were garments evoking periods from fashion's history, from floor-length evening dresses in black satin to long-sleeved wool dresses with appliqué decoration. At Abingdon Road, Hulanicki designed her first Thirties-inspired dress, a 'long satin dress with bra-style bodice and narrow diamanté shoulder straps', on sale for £6 6s (opposite).[23] The past was ever-present in Hulanicki's design and in the Biba look.

To run the boutique, Hulanicki and Fitz-Simon employed Sarah Plunkett, a former *vendeuse* at the British couture house Bellville. Liz Dickson, editor of *Queen* magazine and an acquaintance of both Barbara and Sarah, made the introductions after Hulanicki expressed the need for a shop manager. 'I was interviewed in one of the Bellville houses in Motcomb Street by Barbara and Fitz!' remembers Plunkett.[24] Her cousin, Rosie Marks, would also go on to work for Hulanicki. 'I was interviewed outside the shop in Abingdon Road,' she recalls. 'Barbara came out and talked about hair and clothes and that sort of thing. I mean, she never asked me if I'd had any experience or could type or do shorthand. I had no idea [what the job was] and Barbara said, "Okay, that's fine, when can you start?" We literally just chatted about fashion – we just clicked. I was wearing a skirt with some white Courrèges-type boots and I had a short haircut, that sort of Vidal Sassoon cut. I think she liked my hair.'[25]

Left: Julie Christie wears a Biba trouser suit in *Darling* (1965)

Opposite: 'Long satin dress with bra-style bodice and narrow diamanté shoulder straps', *Woman's Mirror*, 2 April 1966. Photo: David Olins.

Two shop assistants also joined. 'These two girls came in from Harrods' export department, these little blonde dollies, Eleanor and Irene,' Hulanicki remembers, 'and Fitz said, "I'm terribly sorry but we can only afford one of you." And they went, "We're not coming then, it's either two of us or nothing", so he said, "Okay, we'll have to take both of you."' Due to lack of space, the workrooms, where pattern cutter Ann Behr and two machinists created the first samples of Hulanicki's designs, were located in Hulanicki and Fitz-Simon's flat on Cromwell Road.

The difficulties encountered sourcing fabric for the mail-order gingham dress influenced Hulanicki's decision to make only 500 of any one design in any one fabric (a policy that was rescinded in 1968 for mail-order catalogues only). The benefits were twofold, in that there was never a shortage of fabric and the shop always looked fresh. The policy did, however, throw up a significant and enduring problem: the sourcing of new fabrics. As was the case with many of Hulanicki's contemporaries, ignorance mixed with enthusiasm often came before business – in the very early days, Hulanicki would buy fabric over the counter, unaware that wholesale was available. The local department store, Pontings on Kensington High Street (right) was a convenient source of fabrics and later a gold mine of undiscovered textile treasures: 'I got to know the guy in the fabric department and he took me to his store, this whole office full of Thirties fabrics – wool crêpes, crêpe de Chine. They were faded, but we used to use lots of those old Pontings fabrics in the early days.'

Burgess Ledward, the company who had provided that desperately needed supply of pink gingham, became a reliable source, with many fabrics from their archive, which had been discontinued by the 1960s, put back into production due solely to the demand from Biba. After a number of years of working with Biba, the textile company even brought a former employee out of retirement to work specifically with Hulanicki on research and the production of discontinued base fabrics. 'We were big time with them because we paid our bills,' Hulanicki explains. 'I was very into vintage stuff: [1930s fabrics and

cottons with Victorian prints such as] crêpe, marocain, crêpe de Chine, flanesta, which was sort of like a copy of Liberty wool but it was in rayon. All these were completely out of fashion by then, so they were digging all this out. They had a fantastic library of their stuff and I would ask for something and they would develop the base fabrics for me. Then the prints – we either [did] them in-house or we would use their old archive prints. At a later stage, we did all the colourways in-house and [had them] printed by Burgess Ledward up in Leicester.'

The production of in-house prints began in the earliest days of the first Biba shop. Interior designer and printer Julie Hodgess, who had met Hulanicki at the opening of shoe designer Moya Bowler's showroom in 1964, remembers producing studio prints, known as 'croquis', for Hulanicki: 'I designed some patterns, little designs for clothes, and some of them got printed. Barbara really loved different [styles] and we had very, very simple printing procedures. Quite a few of them were made up into her garments.'[26]

Opposite: Biba daisy-print ensemble, c.1965, Photo: Peter Atherton.

Right: Advert for Derrys (later the site of Big Biba, see p.163 onwards), Barkers and Pontings stores on Kensington High Street, 1951

From her workroom, Hodgess would print fabrics with simple screen prints, usually in a single colour, thus creating unique Biba prints in very limited runs. For larger runs, in-house designs would be printed by IVO Prints, a firm of textile and wallpaper printers established in 1963. '[The fabrics] used to come back stiff like a board and stinking of printing ink. We would get them to print on base fabrics and I'd do the colourways for the designs,' Hulanicki recalls. 'There was only one colourway, wasn't there? Purple, purple and purple.' IVO Prints would go on to work with designers including Ossie Clark, Zandra Rhodes and Vivienne Westwood.

The distinctive Biba prints were matched by the unique fit of the clothes, which unwittingly created exclusivity. Biba clothes may have been affordable for the many, but the ultra-skinny fit was suitable only for the few. Hulanicki introduced a unique shape into fashion and a new silhouette to fashion history: horizontal shoulders, long torso, bustless and waistless, with armholes placed high up the torso. Curvy or sporty girls were unable to wear Biba clothes, which were so tight-fitting that even the girls who could fit into them were unable to lift their arms to any useful degree. For added tightness on the sleeves, Hulanicki included a small dart at the elbow, eliminating any fabric bulges when the arm was straightened.

If the fit of the clothes was remarkable, the Biba colours were a revelation: dark, sombre and funereal, in contrast to the light, bright Pop art colours of contemporary fashion. Plum, mulberry, prune, brown and purple were the quintessential Biba shades. They were also known to Hulanicki as 'Auntie' colours in reference to her Aunt Sophie's preferred colour palette – as the soubriquet suggests, Biba colours were pure nostalgia. 'They were very Alphonse Mucha, Klimt, that period. They were Art Nouveau colours, which I loved,' Hulanicki explains.

In combining unique fit, distinctive colours and unusual prints, Barbara Hulanicki created a particular look for her customers and a characteristic identity, that of the Biba Dolly. Auntie's life in couture was influencing the Biba look, *was* the Biba look, but made available by Hulanicki to the girl in the street. Other companies of the period produced inexpensive clothes aimed at the young. In 1963, the success of Mary Quant's Bazaar boutique on the King's Road led her to manufacture her designs wholesale under the Ginger Group label. These garments were sold in retail outlets nationwide and in America through the J.C. Penney chain of department stores. The Dutch company C&A also successfully sold clothes to teenage, fashion-conscious Londoners in the early 1960s, with the occasional, limited, range of designs from the continent. Mainstream retailers, however, had neither the desire nor the vision to take the market seriously and continued to produce mismatching separates, or, as Janey Ironside called them, 'desperates'.[27]

If Mary Quant's Bazaar was 'a sort of permanently running cocktail party', Biba was a non-stop Fellini film.[28] A Biba dress or outfit represented something radically new and, for many teenagers, the first visit to Abingdon Road was a revelation. 'I was 15 when I first discovered Biba,' recalls Annie Hawker, who went to school in west London at the time. 'I must have read about it, and I remember finding this little shop and in there was just this amazing small selection of dresses and clothes, but very cheap. This fantastic trouser suit with fabulous patterns on – I'd never seen anything like it before.'[29] A Biba dress transformed the way girls like Annie saw and felt about themselves and Biba became their shop of choice: 'After discovering such an amazing place, which was affordable, you wouldn't want to go anywhere else. You couldn't even compare it to anywhere else because there was nothing that was interesting or new and different on the high street.'[30]

If the clothes ushered in a new way for young women to dress, the store transformed the way that people shopped. From the beginning of Biba, it was Hulanicki's intention for the clothes to be theatrical, making each girl into 'a Hollywood film star'. The shop was merely an extension of this fantasy. A former chemist's shop, 87 Abingdon Road had been left empty for a number of years. Hulanicki retained the chipped and peeling paint of the exterior – the hint of dereliction instantly conveying the building's age but also ringing a low note before the high of the interior, the black-and-white before the Technicolor in the *Wizard of Oz* (1939). Biba was, if nothing else, about drama. The interior aimed to be a cinematic version of a drawing room or nightclub, a louche setting to be explored.

Grace Coddington in the Biba shop, 87 Abingdon Road, London, *Boutique* (c.1965). Photo: Marc Hispard.

Two huge windows at the front and the side of the building exposed the interior to a large amount of light, although this was initially obscured by two signs carrying the new Biba logo, designed by John McConnell, with the addition a short time later of a heavy crêpe curtain. (This came down almost as quickly as it went up and was replaced by lace attached to the windowpane itself, as Hulanicki explains: 'We sold this mail-order dress in the same fabric as the curtain and then we ran out of fabric, so we had to take the curtain down for the orders.')

Julie Hodgess contributed wallpaper to the shop: a swirling Art Nouveau-inspired design in black and gold, as a backdrop for the shop-as-set. Aspects of the interior design at Abingdon Road would become Biba classics, with some elements becoming synonymous with the name. Bentwood hatstands were adopted as a cheap and easy method of hanging the clothes, but became associated with the store to the extent that they were used in every incarnation of Biba. Palms adorned the floors, planted in

Victorian jardinières bought for a few pounds at second-hand shops in London and Brighton. Black-and-white tiles covered the floor, a look Hulanicki borrowed from the banqueting scene in Sergei Eisenstein's film *Ivan the Terrible, Part II* (1958). Feather boas in florid colours also became a hallmark of Biba and, although originally employed as props to dress the hatstands, were soon found around the necks of Biba girls (and some boys).

Communal changing rooms became not only a Biba signature but also a sector standard for retailers up until the 1980s. Again, their origins were happy accident rather than calculated design. 'We put up screens [for people to

Below: Julie Hodgess, drawing of abstract floral pattern for printed Biba textile, work on paper, c.1965

Opposite, above: Barbara Hulanicki in the Biba shop, 87 Abingdon Road, London, c.1965

Opposite, below: Interior of Biba, 87 Abingdon Road, London, c.1965. Photo: Roy Milligan.

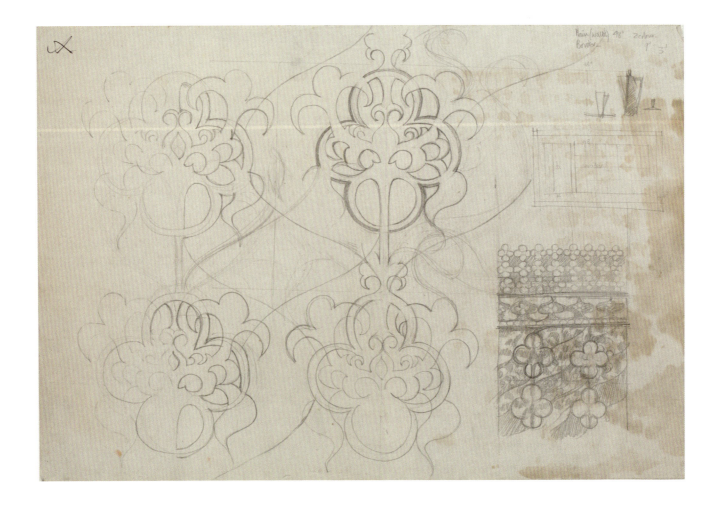

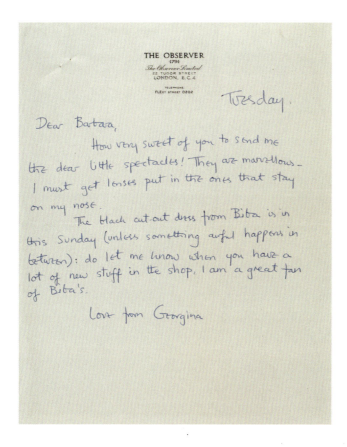

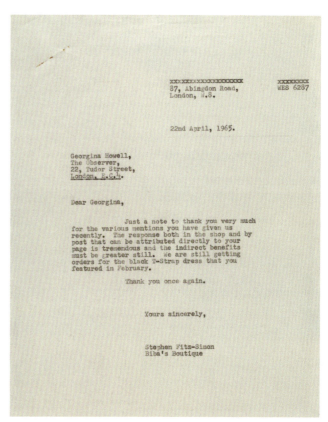

Opposite: Biba shop interior, 87 Abingdon Road, London, c.1965. Photo: Ray Milligan.

Above: Correspondence between Georgina Howell at the *Observer*, Barbara Hulanicki and Stephen Fitz-Simon, 1965

change behind],' Hulanicki recalls. 'They would throw the clothes over the screen and you'd get an amount of clothes and the screen would fall down and they'd take no notice and just keep changing in the shop full of boys!' Where Biba led, others followed. 'In the Harrods new Way-In boutique there are communal changing rooms,' the *Sun* reported in 1967. 'This is another method by which the new casual boutique shops, including the famous Biba's [sic] in Kensington, are preventing shoplifting.'[31]

Shoplifting was an issue for Biba from the beginning, perhaps 'encouraged' by the relaxed attitude of staff, dim lighting and the customer demographic. 'It's the worst of our problems,' Hulanicki said some years later.

'On our opening day we lost 103 pairs of earrings, 78 pairs of sunglasses and God knows what else. That was just the opening!'[32] Theft wasn't a problem unique to Biba. 'We had a terrible problem with thieves, terrible. More stuff was stolen than sold,' James Wedge, owner of the clothing boutiques Top Gear and Countdown on the King's Road, remembers. 'I sold fur coats, which were very expensive, so I put a chain through the sleeve and round the rail and padlocked them. I went out to lunch, came back and there were three chains hanging and the coats were gone. They must have slit the blimmin' sleeves and took them.'[33]

Real fur was to make an appearance in Hulanicki's designs from winter 1965 though to the spring of 1967. However, achieving the Biba look in real fur at affordable prices was to be a challenge too far for Hulanicki and Fitz-Simon. To keep costs down, the fur 'pelts' were constructed from rectangular off-cuts measuring approximately 8 x 10 cm, and the garments' seams were

minimal – fur did not have the 'give' of woven materials, and so the results were ripped seams and damaged garments. 'I wanted the coats to be very narrow, really tight on the arms,' Hulanicki recalls, 'which, if you look at most fur coats, is not usual … When the coats came in, of course, when people tried them on, the arms just fell away.' Instead, with excellent examples of fake fur widely available on the market, Biba fur was no longer real from 1967 onwards (with the exception of the Biba couture range made from 1969 to 1971).

Biba was a product of its era and, like other successful designers of the period, Hulanicki was able to predict and, to some extent, prescribe what the public would be wearing. 'Everybody's on the same wavelength [because of] what they're reading and watching. You know very well how they're thinking and it's your decision to put it in the shop and it's their decision if they're going to buy it. It's fair play on both sides,' she explains. 'You only don't know [if something will sell] if it's a new thing completely, but then with a shop you can ease it in slowly, say you're doing a new shape or something. You just get on the wheel of fashion. You've got to be on that wheel, not too far ahead and not too late – to time yourself so you're just that moment ahead.' The long-sleeved T-shirt, which became an early Biba classic and remained in production for the whole of the company's life, was very nearly a casualty of being too far ahead. Made in jersey, these T-shirts were manufactured by Vedonis, a Leicester-based company that had started out in the 1800s, making men's underwear. Hulanicki's designs, dyed in a range of Biba colours, sat on the shelves of Abingdon Road without a sale: 'Nothing happened and then suddenly Ernestine Cater [fashion editor of *The Times*] featured a drawing of jerseys and they just flew out.' The ability to anticipate the market was not understood by all of Biba's partners. 'Our first fashion T-shirt was the rugby one, cotton striped with a white collar,' Hulanicki says. '[They were] made from a real rugby T-shirt by Admiral, who were quite small then. The Admiral reps came in late one evening and I told them I wanted this shape – I want the T-shirts like this, da-da-da – and they were laughing and being really rude, so Fitz came up and growled at them. Then we gave them a huge order and there was complete silence.'

Biba 'Admiral' dress, c.1965. Photo: Ron Falloon.

Biba evolved through innovation and experimentation, successes and the occasional failure. An association with Brigitte Bardot and the world of celebrity had contributed to the success of the pink gingham dress, and now Vicki Wickham, producer of the television programme *Ready, Steady, Go!*, would provide Biba with bona fide celebrity endorsement in the figures of television presenter Cathy McGowan and singer Cilla Black. *Ready, Steady, Go!* was launched in August 1963 and hosted by the teenage McGowan. Ostensibly a music programme, *Ready, Steady, Go!* aired every Friday at 5.30 p.m. on ITV and launched McGowan's career, earning her the title 'Queen of the Mods'. As a representative of her generation, what McGowan said, did and, more importantly, wore, were emulated by thousands of young girls across the country. McGowan herself became a Biba fanatic and wore either Biba or Foale & Tuffin for her Friday-night appearances. Hulanicki recalls their first meeting at TV studios in Holborn: 'We got on like a house on fire. She liked my man's watch. She was just amazing looking. She had incredible taste for someone her age – terribly elegant, long legs, great hair.'

Cilla Black was also among the first celebrities to wear and enthusiastically promote Biba. Along with McGowan, she could often be found at the workrooms in Cromwell Road: 'By my late teens, Biba was the top of my list. I was friends with its owner [and] I would sit in her flat as she made the clothes Cathy McGowan and I would wear on TV's *Ready, Steady, Go!*'[34] Other celebrities were to follow: the boutique was visited regularly by Mick Jagger with his then girlfriend Chrissie Shrimpton (sister of model Jean), Jane Asher, Sonny and Cher, Julie Christie, and Twiggy, with her boyfriend Justin de Villeneuve. 'Twiggy used to come in, in those days, in her school uniform,' shop manager Sarah Plunkett remembers. 'Perhaps [Justin] bought her the odd [outfit] to wear, which she looked amazing in. There were a lot of those chicks that used to come in and looked fantastic. Barbara just got it right, and there [were] a lot of skinnies around.'[35]

Another memorable visitor in 1965 was artist Yoko Ono. A forthcoming television appearance had brought Ono into Biba to buy a dress. Hulanicki's assistant, Rosie Marks, spent time choosing a suitable dress with Ono, only to see it shredded on television later that evening. Ono's performance

They're CRISP!.. Clothes the Clan are raving about ...Designed for Elkie Brooks, they're coming at your price!

Barbara Hulanicki's designs are really crisp! But Cilla and I agree, she's a problem. Why? Because she's so good we'd like to keep her to ourselves—our "secret" dressmaker. On the other hand, she deserves to be wider known. We just *have* to tell other people about her.

Like Cilla, I introduced Barbara to Elkie Brooks at the Ad Lib. It was just before Elkie was to go to New York with the Animals. She wasn't happy with her clothes and Barbara promised to design some specially for the trip.

They were so super I asked her if I could show them to **rave** readers. And here they are! Elkie's wearing them.

Barbara is Britain's top fashion artist, so I was delighted when she agreed to do the sketches herself. Designing such great clothes is a fairly new development for her. Now she's taken the great plunge, gone into manufacturing and opened her own little boutique in Kensington.

Barbara is making copies of Elkie's clothes, so you can wear them, too. And they're ridiculously cheap now they're in production. I don't know how she does it! There's more on page 38.

For those cool Clan parties, simplicity is the style. Like this long dress in black and white pin dot jerseyland at £3 3s. Sizes 8-14. Looks great!

Still on easy-on-eye simplicity, this black crepe tube dress with full-length flared sleeves and beach bobble turning at neck and cuffs takes a lot of beating. Cost: £3 3s. Sizes 8-16.

Always get your man in one of these two-piece suits; patterned lace (left), white rib (below), with matching shoes by Saxone. Suit sizes 8-14 at £5 5s. For that ice-cool Clan look top the suit with a matching hat: £1 1s

of her work *Cut Piece* (first performed in 1964 in Tokyo) involved inviting audience members to take scissors to her clothes, eventually leaving the artist in her underwear. '[Rosie] thought Fitz was going to fire her the next day,' Hulanicki says.

Ono had been introduced to Biba by her friend, the poet and provocateur Jill Richter. Together with her husband, the performer and dancer Daniel Richter (who later played the ape in the opening sequence of Stanley Kubrick's 1968 film *2001: A Space Odyssey*) and John Eason, Jill Richter organized the first Beat poetry readings at the Royal Albert Hall, with performers including Allen Ginsberg, Adrian Mitchell and Gregory Corso. For her wedding at Marylebone registry office in June 1965, she made the

35

Your man will envy this "Carnaby" shirt on a casual date. In white or black crepe, it costs £2 2s. Wear with 5s pearl links (below).

Ideal for slim Clan-girls: this delicate "Cathy" smock dress priced at £3 3s in navy and white dot jerseyland with white pique collar and cuffs. The soft hat costs £1 1s.

Clan-wear accessories: a 5 ft-long scarf and matching hat in black-white check. Hat: £1 1s. Scarf: 19s 6d.

HANDS UP!

JRES BY P. L. JAMES

Cathy McGowan, 'Clan Clothes For You', with illustrations by Barbara Hulanicki and photographs showing Elkie Brooks modelling Biba clothes, *Rave* (November 1964)

ourselves.'[36] The article (left) featured six outfits modelled by singer Elkie Brooks, including a Courrèges-style two-piece suit in lace (£5 5s), an empire-line dress (£3 3s) and a long-sleeved jumpsuit in printed cotton (£4 4s). It also included two outfits in crêpe, a signature Biba fabric: a plain black tube dress with flared sleeves, and a shirt that was available in black or white. The shirt's upstanding Eton collar was also a signature Biba style, dating back to Hulanicki's design for the *Evening Standard* competition of 1955, and continued to appear on her clothes through to the end of the 1960s.

The quality of Hulanicki's designs attracted a wider demographic than just teenagers. The groundbreaking magazine *Nova*, launched in 1965, was aimed squarely at twenty-somethings. An article in the July 1965 issue, titled 'Dressing on the Breadline', brought together 55 outfits for those on a budget and contained advice for the uninitiated: 'Some of the happiest hunting grounds just now for cheap clothes are the postal boutiques … call it inexpensive if you like but I call it cheap.'[37] Two Biba outfits were included: a trouser suit for 5gns and a suit for 4gns, with matching hat and scarf (1gn). Dresses by Simon Ellis (four-and-a-half gns), Mary Quant (four-and-a-half gns) and Caroline Charles (5gns) were also included, as was a blazer by Slimma (£3 19s 11d) and shoes by Freeman, Hardy and Willis (£2 9s).

Stephen Fitz-Simon always focused on keeping the price of Biba clothes as low as possible, cutting production costs to the bare minimum, to the extent that Biba labels were not included inside garments for the first four years of the company's life.

Biba clothes may have been inexpensive, but Hulanicki's philosophy was for the Biba look itself to be as expensive as possible. Matching outfits were a hallmark of Biba and Hulanicki designed entire ensembles, with a dress, hat, bag and shoes, all in coordinated fabrics – an idea that had never before been attempted on the high street: 'I was always interested in "matchy-matchy" from the beginning. My mother used to have matchy-matchy [outfits] and [as children] we had to have all our little dresses with matchy-

unconventional choice of wearing a printed Biba jumpsuit, a matching hat and some plastic beads.

In November 1964, Cathy McGowan highlighted Biba in her regular column in *Rave* magazine, a publication aimed at the female teenage market: 'Barbara Hulanicki's designs are really crisp! But Cilla and I agree, she's a problem. Why? Because she's so good we'd like to keep her to matchy knickers and matchy-matchy hats.' With printed fabrics, the process for 'matchy-matchy' was relatively straightforward, with each manufacturer making their respective item – dress, hat, bag – in the same fabric design. For a whole range of products to be produced in Biba colours, however, the work involved was phenomenal. 'There was no Pantone [colour reference system] then, so you'd have people sitting there painting out sheets of colour to send to the manufacturers,' Hulanicki recalls. 'They'd go by the colour you sent them and that was just for the one colour – multiply that by 23 [colours] and loads of products. It was terribly important because that meant *expensive* to me, and nobody else would do it because it was a lot of work. That look was the expensive look.'

Accessories were integral in creating the Biba look and footwear was essential. 'Shoes were always big for Biba and you needed them to finish the picture,' Hulanicki explains. '[In Britain], because of the war, the girls were brought up wearing one pair of shoes until they fell off. They would wear one pair with everything, until they dropped off. That part of their outfit was a disaster.' Hats were also intrinsic to Biba's 'matchy-matchy' look, as demonstrated even by the simple, triangular, pink gingham headscarf that formed part of the postal boutique's first success. The early hats for the boutique were made by the painter Molly Parkin (who would go on to become an award-winning fashion editor) from Hulanicki's designs, which were influenced by her childhood: 'We used to wear these little Christopher Robin hats as children, which were really sweet, so I just designed some and had Molly make them for the shop.'

Jewellery was supplied by Adrian Mann, but some additional pieces were foisted on to Hulanicki who, against her better judgement, attempted to sell them in her shop. She remembers Anjelica Huston, then a 14-year-old schoolgirl, visiting Biba with Joan Buck, the future fashion editor of French *Vogue*: 'I don't know why, but I was terrified of them. They were at school and they used to come in and flog me these Art Deco buttons they made out of, I don't know, chewing gum! They had safety pins on the back, which used to fall off, but I was so scared of them I used to buy them. Eventually Fitz said, "Will you please stop buying these stupid things."' Huston admitted in her 2013 memoirs that she and her friend would 'pore over

the racks of dresses and stuff a few under our uniforms, and on the way out we'd check the velvet ottoman in the centre of the floor to see if there were any rejects [left by previous customers] worthy of inclusion.'[38]

Biba's landlord would also 'persuade' Hulanicki to sell his beads: 'He was a rep for a really big jewellery company, which, luckily, did really nice plastic beads, which looked like ivory. He lived under the shop and we were so worried he was going to ask us to put carpet down, which would have ruined the whole image, that we had to put all his stuff in the shop.'

The democratic ideals of the era – the bedrock of the Biba philosophy – saw the postal boutique extend its reach during the Abingdon Road years with the launch of the first Biba catalogue. This was the first vehicle Hulanicki used to create, in print, the complete Biba look – face, clothes, accessories and attitude (opposite). Sent to existing customers who were already on the company's order books and those potential customers generated by Biba's continual presence in magazines such as *Petticoat*, *Rave* and *Honey*, the catalogue also represented the first attempt to take the Biba look to audiences outside London. Illustrated with Hulanicki's wide-eyed 'Cathy McGowans' and Shrimpton-esque girls, the catalogue offered dresses for £3, hats at 21s and bags for 37s 6d. Included for sale in one catalogue was the 'Dolly Dress' (opposite, top-right), a smock in grey flannel for £3 3s.

The smock was a signature style for Biba through to the company's final years, and a key look for the 1960s. The smock's associations with childhood made it the perfect garment to express fashion's obsession with youth, and almost every designer and manufacturer interested in capturing this market produced a version. A fashion feature in *Petticoat* magazine offered a 'Navy/white smock made with short puff sleeves banded on a tight cuff' by Simon Massey for 99s 11d, a 'pink gingham stolen from a pretty table cloth, sewn into a high-line no-sleeved dress' by Lee Cecil for 99s 6d, and an 'all day and every

Details from Biba catalogue with illustrations by Barbara Hulanicki, March 1965: (clockwise from top-left) 'Empire Line Dress – grey and white Welsh flannel'; 'DOLLY DRESS – grey flannel'; 'T-STRAP – black blended wool'; 'Black Corduroy jacket, with flaired [sic] skirt/ Matching hat/ flaired [sic] pants'

Empire Line Dress - grey and white Welsh flannel.

Short sleeves with pearl buttons - £3. 10s. 0d.

gently flaired skirt.

Hat to match - 21s. 0d.

EMPIRE LINE DRESS - grey flannel - long sleeves - pearl button on cuff. £3. 3s. 0d.

Matching hat - 21s. 0d.

DOLLY DRESS - grey flannel - funnel sleeves lace trimmed collar and cuffs. £3. 3s. 0d.

Black Corduroy Jacket. With flaired skirt - £7. 7s. 0d.

Matching hat - 21s. 0d.

With flaired pants - £8. 8s. 0d.

T-STRAP - black blended wool. £2. 15s. 0d.

Drop earrings - crystal, black and tortoiseshell. 9s. 3d.

day smock dress in pure white scattered with fresh grown petal spots' by Rhona Roy for 7gns.[39] Also included were smocks by Neatawear (5gns) and Hildebrand (8gns). Paper patterns offered the home dressmaker the cheapest, if not easiest, alternative. A number of Le-Roy patterns of the period were illustrated though not designed by Hulanicki (above).

A more concrete method of bringing Biba to a wider audience arrived at the end of 1965. Hulanicki and Fitz-Simon opened a branch of Biba in her old home town of Brighton, in a shop conveniently located halfway down the main road from the station to the seafront. On Saturday, 29 October 1965, 21 Queen's Road, a small Regency house with a retail space on the ground floor, became the second Biba boutique (opposite). 'Inside the shop it's like a cross between a jungle and a cavern.

Above, left: Le-Roy paper dressmaking pattern 3156 with illustration by Barbara Hulanicki, Britain, c.1964

Above, right: 'Biba' editorial, *Rave* (September 1965). Photo: P.L. James.

Purple art-nouveau wallpaper (hand-printed especially for [Hulanicki]) blooms over the walls,' a local newspaper revealed. 'She'll be selling dresses no dearer than £3 10s.; coats of many colours in shimmering cloth for around £11, with matching trousers; skinny dresses like elongated vests for 18 bob.'[40] One Brighton resident and Biba shopper recalls, 'It was definitely the coolest place to be in Brighton. It was very small, it was very dark, it seemed to be filled with things that we'd never seen before.'[41]

The rapidly growing company became all-encompassing, reflecting changes in Hulanicki and Fitz-Simon's lives.

Above: Biba at 21 Queen's Road, Brighton, c.1966

Overleaf: Biba staff moving stock from 87 Abingdon Road, c.1966

Running four separate premises – the London and Brighton boutiques, offices in Motcomb Street, workrooms in Cromwell Road – *and* the postal-boutique business was turning into a logistical nightmare, as the Biba baby grew at an ever-increasing rate. 'You were just at it day and night, night and day, the energy just moving things along,' Hulanicki says of that time. A move was the only way to bring some sanity back to their lives and to fulfill their company's potential. Abingdon Road, a ground for experimentation, was the crucible for all that Biba was to become. Many elements would never leave Abingdon Road, but many more would continue on to the next stage of Biba.

Right: Biba, striped cotton dress, Britain, c.1965

Opposite, left: Biba, striped wool dress with collar, Britain, c.1965

Opposite, right: Biba, woven floral jersey dress with black sleeves, Britain, c.1965

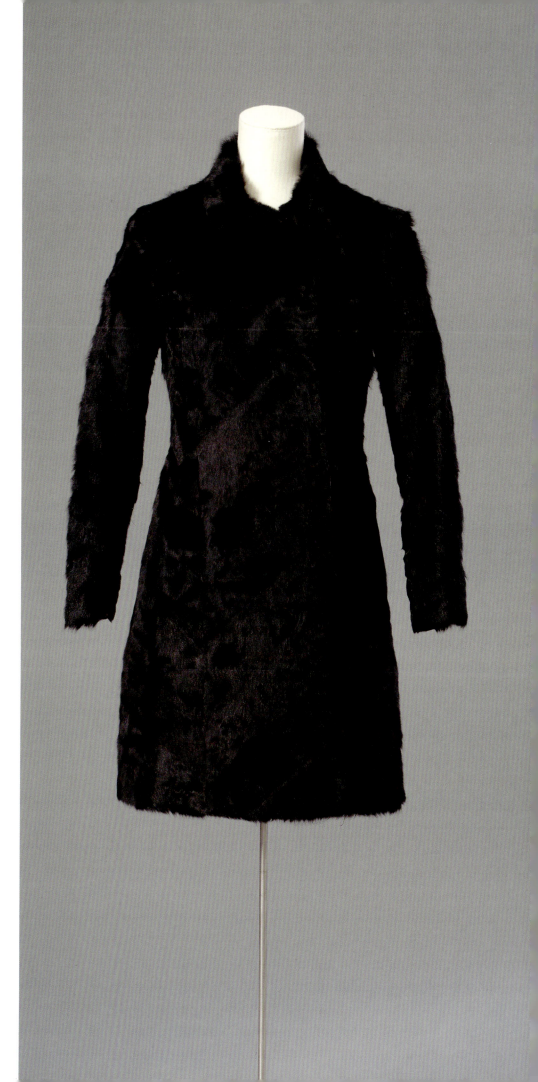

'This would have been the first narrow fur coat, because fur coats were usually these horrible old-fashioned coats with big sleeves. This is fitted, very fitted!'

Opposite, left: Biba, printed cotton jacket, Britain, 1965

Opposite, right: Biba, corduroy coat, Britain, 1965

Right: Biba, rabbit- and goat's-fur coat, Britain, c.1966

'When people like something they need mark I, mark II and mark III. A progression.'

Left: Biba, daisy-print cotton jumpsuit and hat, Britain, 1965

Opposite, left: Biba, Art Nouveau-print cotton maxi dress, Britain, 1964

Opposite, right: Biba, woven cotton maxi dress, Britain, 1964

Left: Biba, chevron-striped cotton voile dress, Britain, 1965

Opposite, left: Biba, linen shift dress, Britain, 1964

Opposite, right: Biba, striped wool smock dress, Britain, c.1964

19–21 Kensington Church Street

1966–1969

'Biba led the way for those of us young girls living in provincial places where we felt we were dying of drabness. She was the first person to introduce colours like mulberry, plum, rust and blueberry ... and she reinvented herringbone tweed, gangster hats and 1930s satins ... to die for.'

Annie Lennox, 2013[1]

In the 16 months that Biba was at Abingdon Road, the name came to be recognized across the country. A constant presence in magazines and regular appearances on television, thanks to Cathy McGowan and Cilla Black, firmly established Biba as part of youth culture. The company's move to larger premises on Kensington Church Street therefore brought nationwide press coverage, with the *Daily Mail* reporting that 'the original, the oldest, the mother of the whole fantastic dolly-gear explosion – [is] moving from its disused chemist's shop in Abingdon Road to new premises in Church Street.'[2] 'Cilla and Co Help Move Shop,' proclaimed the *Daily Mirror*, accompanied by a picture of Black and McGowan clambering out of a van with the necessary, and not so necessary, fittings for the new premises (opposite). The *Daily Mirror*, a newspaper whose circulation reached five million in the 1960s, was covering a London boutique that had existed for less than a year and a half.[3] The media interest was a testament to the success of Barbara Hulanicki's vision and Stephen Fitz-Simon's business acumen and, with the new shop at Kensington Church Street, Biba would become *the* fashion label that represented 'Swinging London', both nationally and internationally.

It had become clear after the first six months that the boutique at Abingdon Road was far too small to accommodate the number of customers Biba was attracting each week. 'It was bursting at the seams and it was almost impossible to sell anything because customers couldn't get to the till,' Hulanicki recalls. On the lookout for new, larger premises, she and Fitz-Simon noticed a vacant triple-

Cilla Black and Cathy McGowan lead the move from 87 Abingdon Road to 19–21 Kensington Church Street, *Daily Mirror*, 28 February 1966

fronted shop on Kensington Church Street. Still empty six months later, the former butcher's and greengrocer's shop was chosen to become the new Biba. There followed a rather unconventional meeting with the shop's owner, Mr Jenkins – an expert in phrenology who believed Fitz-Simon to have 'one of the most interesting heads' he had ever seen. 'You are bound to be a success – the store is yours,' Mr Jenkins told him.[4]

Work began on creating the new shop. The site was to combine retail space and offices, with workrooms still located off-site at Hulanicki and Fitz-Simon's home – now a flat on Exhibition Road in South Kensington. The new location allowed the couple to extend the Biba philosophy, as all manner of products could now be accommodated. 'Biba started the boutique boom,' reported the *Evening News*. 'Now, at the height of fashion's frenzy to buy beat clothes in the "little shops," the boutique that began it all is blazing a new trail for the breakaways. To-day, Biba the boutique is closed. For good. Instead, lock stock and pops, they've moved into a Pocket Store – the first of its kind in London.'[5]

Much of the original early-twentieth-century interior at Kensington Church Street was retained, including the magnificent wall-to-wall mahogany shelving (overleaf). 'It had a huge dresser unit with a clock on one of the walls,'

Above: Revised Biba logo designed by Antony Little, 1966

Below: Shop manager Eleanor Powell outside Biba, 19-21 Kensington Church Street, London, c.1967

Opposite: Shop assistants (from left: Michelle and Nicole Hellier, and Susy and Rosy Young) at Biba, 19-21 Kensington Church Street, London, c.1967. Photo: Caroline Gillies.

interior designer Julie Hodgess remembers. The shop was given a contemporary feel with another of her designs: 'I did a wallpaper for there, which was red background, gold again, and hot – the whole mood was hot. There was a basement area, and we made a wooden balustrade to create the open dressing room, which was wonderful because everybody was pretty exposed to the rest of the world. I think they did try and stop fellas going down a bit, but ...'[6]

The black-and-white tiled floor inspired by *Ivan the Terrible* was again employed, as was the dark interior, which would become a hallmark of all Biba shops. This was created not with lace or heavy curtains as at Abingdon Road, but with household paint. Antony Little, a young designer and illustrator, had first worked for Biba when he assisted Julie Hodgess with the installation of her wallpaper at the previous shop. Like Hulanicki, Little was a convert to the Art Nouveau aesthetic and especially interested in the work of Aubrey Beardsley (1872–98). Beardsley, who died at the age of 25 from tuberculosis, left behind a body of work that was still considered shocking more than 60 years after his death. Young, talented and doomed, he became a totemic figure for the 1960s youth generation, and an exhibition of his works at the Victoria and Albert Museum in the summer of 1966 helped to establish Beardsley as 'the new hero in London'.[7] Little designed the new, Art Nouveau-inspired, black-and-gold logo for Church Street (p.72), which was painted across the three windows of the new shop (overleaf), leaving only small apertures of plain glass to peer through. 'We painted the windows,' Hulanicki recalls, 'and we were a bit ignorant because there was more paint than glass, and when it got hot – pow! One of the windows exploded.' Hulanicki also used Little's designs on Biba stock. 'She used to go through my sketchbooks regularly and she'd make a mark with a yellow asterisk next to the ones she liked, either for textiles or wallpapers,' Little says. 'I'd then draw them up properly and she'd buy them for, I think, £10 a design.'[8]

Black and gold became the unofficial colours of Biba marketing. 'It was based on the old funeral parlour that was over the other side of the road. I loved the severity of the look and also its timelessness,' Hulanicki explains. A diary decorated with Little's logo in the Biba colours

Opposite: Shoppers at the counter of Biba, 19-21 Kensington Church Street, London, 1967

Above: Antony Little, drawings for the exterior of Biba at 19-21 Kensington Church Street, London, work on paper, January 1966

Overleaf: Sandie Shaw sees a passer-by through the window of Biba, 19-21 Kensington Church Street, London, c.1966

was sold in the shop in 1967 (p.78). The very first Biba-branded 'product', it was also a subconscious attempt to evoke a Biba lifestyle, with a list at the back of the book of restaurants and theatres Biba customers might wish to visit. Intended as recommendations for overseas visitors unfamiliar with London, it became a list of unofficial Biba haunts, where one could mingle with like-minded people.

Biba, branded diary and notebook, Britain, 1967

The influence of the decorative arts of the interwar period was to become more obvious in Hulanicki's designs in the Church Street years. 'At the moment it's the 30's [sic] that fascinate me,' she said in a 1966 interview. 'I wallow in old books and the films they've been showing on TV. It's the glamour of nostalgia I suppose.'[9] Her use of 1930s fabrics such as crêpe and satin weaves at Abingdon Road was extended to the use of prints of the period. Interest in the Art Deco style had been slowly growing in Britain since the early 1960s and was given further impetus by, first, the 1966 exhibition *Les Années '25': Art Deco/*

Bauhaus/Stijl/Esprit Nouveau held at the Musée des Arts Décoratifs in Paris and, later, the publication in Britain of Bevis Hillier's book *Art Deco of the '20s and '30s* (1968).

Celia Birtwell, the textile designer and wife of fashion designer Ossie Clark, was experimenting with Art Deco styles in 1967, creating prints that evoked British ceramics of the 1920s. That same year the 1930s look began to go mainstream, as *The Times* reported: 'At last week's Associated Fashion Designers' show, muddy crêpes, sagging cardigans and dropped skirts were loudly acclaimed as the new "thirties" look. But the only designers who deserve commercial success are those who adapt as well as adopt pre-war styles, so that the effect is fashion rather than fancy dress. The two outfits [which] present the best of the decade [are a] wool jersey dress with gathered shoulders, £4 10s from Biba ... [and a] grey jersey trouser suit with belted "Jean Brodie" jacket and wide trousers, £13 2s 6d. from Foale and Tuffin.'[10] (Note the significant difference in price.)

A Biba blouse in synthetic silk (p.112) with a geometric 1920s design (probably from the archives of Burgess Ledward) exemplifies the prints now seen as classic Biba, which Hulanicki used in her designs until 1974. The construction of the blouse is also typical, its tight fit achieved with two design and construction details. The puffed sleeve head of the garment is in fact designed to accommodate the wearer's shoulder, rather than sitting on top of it, bringing the armhole tight against the armpit. With a tiny seam from neckline to shoulder, measuring just nine centimetres, the garment also gives the added illusion of skinniness. Unlike the conventional straight dart, the Biba bust dart was shaped like an inverted tick. This allowed additional tightness to be achieved, with the upper dart accommodating the bust while the side dart eradicated additional fabric underneath.

A pivotal moment for London fashion and for Biba came on 15 April 1966 with the publication in the United States of the latest issue of *Time*, the weekly news magazine. Its cover, a cartoon montage that included bug-eyed girls and a grotesque Harold Wilson waving a Union flag, declared 'London: The Swinging City'. The 13-page article contrasted the British establishment with its *demi-monde*; the 'Stately, unchanging, Britannic' with 'Carnaby Street ... What's Happening in London Fashion.'[11] Vidal Sassoon,

Julie Christie, Foale & Tuffin and Cathy McGowan all made appearances, as did a large colour image of the interior of Biba, showing young female shoppers, a table covered in plastic jewellery and bentwood hatstands heaving with clothing. 'Big among boutiques is Biba's [sic] on Kensington Church Street. "Biba" is the nickname of the proprietress' sister,' the caption stated.[12] Included in the article, for the uninitiated, was a map of 'The Scene' (below), centred on central and west London, and, for the even less well informed, there was also a map of England, indicating the position of London. Hulanicki recalls being sceptical about *Time*'s visit in 1966: 'Hello, where have you been all this time?! It started in 1964 with Vicky Wickham and the *Ready, Steady, Go!* lot … They were photographing all across London. It was like, Come on, we've already done it, we're doing it, and you've just discovered it.'

The publication of the magazine, and the resulting national and international interest in London fashion and Biba that followed, helped change Hulanicki's mind: 'When it came out it was amazing – the whole world was suddenly interested. Workmen in the street were whistling at the girls in the skirts.' The *Time* article may have missed the boat by a few years, but what it lacked in accuracy it made up for in effect. The international press recognized London as a world leader in innovative fashion and the global media descended on the city. 'Three Russian models … were visiting London to promote their country's folk fashion,' the *Daily Mirror* reported in May 1967. 'When taken to Biba, one of the models, Ala, looked a little amazed in her modest knee-touching skirt yesterday.

Below: 'The Scene', map of London featured in *Time*, 15 April 1966

Overleaf, left: Model wearing Biba 'Pugin'-print dress, *De Volkskrant*, 6 May 1967

Overleaf, right: Model wearing Biba coat dress, *De Volkskrant*, 6 May 1967

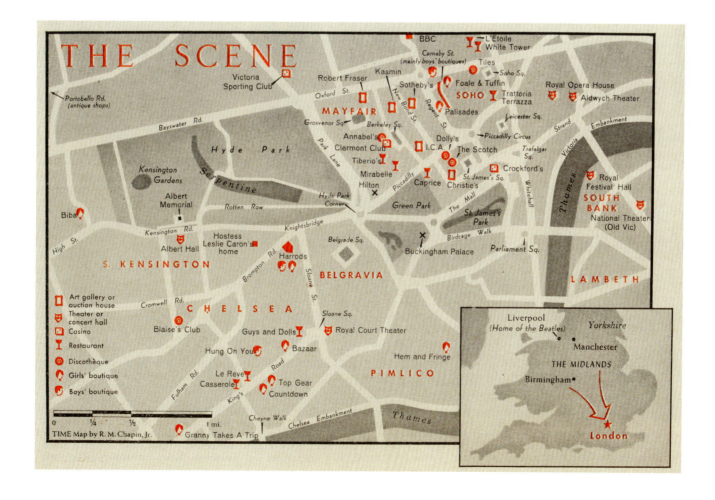

For one thing, Ala discovered that British girls really DO wear skirts that short ... Ala said, "We like the bright colours, but we wouldn't wear most of these clothes in Russia. Russian women are more conservative, shy and modest. These clothes would attract too much attention."[13]

With so much press attention, Biba became more than a shop. In *Petticoat* magazine's regular 'Letter from London' feature, the fictional Maureen tells an overseas friend, 'I've been to Biba's [sic]; you know the boutique we all used to hear so much about? It's a big tourist attraction now, apart from having super clobber. Saturday mornings it's packed out.' She adds, 'If you're not careful, someone might mistake the clothes you've taken off as Biba gear, and leap off with it to the cash desk.'[14]

No longer a small boutique visited by the fashion elite and those in the know, the triple-fronted shop, a stone's throw from Kensington High Street, became a mecca for anyone wanting to experience Swinging London. Brigitte Bardot made an appearance (stripping down to her bra and knickers in a corridor, much to Fitz-Simon's enjoyment), Mia Farrow bought a dress and her then husband Frank Sinatra ordered hats in every Biba colour, which were never paid for; most unexpectedly, Princess Anne paid a visit; and Diana Dors visited the shop (stealing items and waiting to be caught – confirming the old adage that any publicity is good publicity).

Stealing was an unavoidable symptom of the shop's success. One rather bold customer exclaimed, 'I love clothes. They're to me what drink and drugs are to other people. I like them because it's a way of advertising myself to men. I spend half my wages here ... Frankly though, if I come here and see something I really like and can't quite afford it, I just nick it.'[15] Others were more imaginative, as fashion editor Barbara Griggs remembers from a visit to Kensington Church Street: 'One of the sales girls comes in and says, "Right, I'm off", and Barbara turns to me and says, "Half our sales staff spend half their time in the law courts giving evidence against shoplifters." A French girl who had been nicked the day before sneaking out of the shop not just with the dress, which she had actually paid for, but also the matching hat and bag ... had the

Interior of Biba, 19–21 Kensington Church Street, London, c.1966

effrontery to say, "In France if you buy the dress they always give you the hat too."'[16]

The dominance of London fashion was met by some with defensive derision – French fashion designer Gabrielle 'Coco' Chanel believed the mini-skirt to be dirty[17] – and by others with outright imitation, as a letter to fashion editor Felicity Green, received in April 1967, indicates:

Philip Redler and Mslle Danielle Taijblun are 21-yrs-old cousins. They are the owners of Biba – the boutiqueye [sic] that opened at 18 Rue de Sèvres in Paris this morning ... "Have you been very much inspired by London boutiques," I asked M. Redler, "by Biba in London for example?" "Oh no," he cried, shocked, "I've never set foot in the London Biba. I have never heard of it till very recently, whereas my cousin and I have been planning this boutique for ages." "Why," I asked, "have you decided to call your shop Biba?" "Oh, that is my cousin's nickname," said M. Redler. "All her friends call her Biba. It's short for Beatrice," ... "I thought you said it was Danielle." "Well," replied, M. Redler, looking at me straight in the eye, "Beatrice is her second name."[18]

Plans *were* made to open an official Biba in Paris, with Fitz-Simon employing a company to locate suitable properties across the French capital. A number of properties were suggested, including shops on the Place des Vosges, rue de Seine, rue des Francs Bourgeois and rue Gregoire de Tours.[19] It was, unfortunately, not to be: the Biba name had already been copyrighted for continental Europe by another manufacturer, leaving Hulanicki and Fitz-Simon as the owners of the British rights only.

At the end of 1966, a (temporary) Biba outlet opened in Switzerland. The invitation had come from Carl Iverson, an American who was launching a 'fashion fortnight' at the Hotel Post in Zermatt. The ski resort played host to a Biba boutique for the first two weeks of 1967. Decked out with all of the now-familiar Biba accoutrements – hatstands, wallpaper and potted palms – this 'pop-up' Biba was manned by the growing Biba team: Sarah Plunkett, Eleanor Powell, twins Rosie and Susie Young, Kim Willmott, Eva Molnar, Susan Dennis, Irena Stachurska and Mary Austin. The fortnight was attended by author Teddy Goldsmit and dancers from *Ready, Steady, Go!*,

IT'S GEAR ON THE ROCKS...

Eleanor Powell, Biba manageress, dancing at the Biba Ball.

THE LAST of the Biba birds flew home this week, after a London fashion blitz on Zermatt, the Swiss ski resort. For two weeks, people from the Biba shop in Kensington Church Street spearheaded a London fashion campaign, established a "branch" shop there, and led residents and tourists in après-ski nightlife at a specially-opened club. JOHN PROSSER was there to take the pictures for *London Look.*

American skier Carl Iveson originated the fashion fortnight. He is based at the Hotel Post, in Zermatt, and asked the Biba people to fly out and open a store for the New Year holiday season. They agreed immediately, and flew out a team of girls, and all the Biba gear, including the distinctive clothes-racks, wallpaper and decor. The finished store in Zermatt was an exact replica of the Ken-

sington Church Street Shop.

The team was headed by Biba general manager Sarah Plunkett and manageress Eleanor Powell. The girls who took over Biba clothes – including lots of silver, glitter dresses and fur coats – were twins Rosie and Suzy Young, Kim Willmott, Eva Molnar, Susan Dennis, Irena Stachurska and Mary Austin.

John Williams, of the British Army ski team, volunteered to parade the streets with a sandwich-board, reading "Visit Biba at the Hotel Post."

The Zermatt Biba store was soon ready for business, with the familiar Biba wallpaper, mirrors, potted palms and merchandise. There was a run on all the fashion lines, including the famous Biba hats.

The club was specially opened to tie in with the fashion

Above: 'It's Gear on the Rocks', *London Look*, 14 January 1967

Opposite: Interior of Barbara Hulanicki and Stephen Fitz-Simon's house at Brunswick Gardens, *House & Garden* (February 1968). Photo: Ray Williams.

with the band The End performing in the venue's nightclub. 'It's Gear on the Rocks', reported the magazine *London Look* (above). 'For two weeks, people from the Biba shop in Kensington Church Street spearheaded a London fashion campaign, established a "branch" shop there, and led residents and tourists in après-ski nightlife at a specially-opened club.'[20]

The Brighton Biba was not faring so well. The shop was beginning to take up more and more of Hulanicki's time, as staffing became problematic and the shop's day-to-day appearance a worry. It had become the focus for Brighton's underworld; not only were large volumes of clothing leaving the shop unpaid for, but an ex-boxer's visit to Fitz-Simon in London, in the hope of 'protecting' the Brighton Biba, brought home the realization that the boutique was no longer a viable part of the business. 'I thought it was lovely and I wouldn't let it go for ages,' Hulanicki remembers. 'The plan was that we were going to do little stores all over the country, until we opened that one. Never again. Thank God we tried it out there first because it was easy to get to. It took so much time worrying. It was like, Oh God, somebody's got to go down there, and nobody would go down because they were having such a great time in London.'

Life took an unexpected turn for Hulanicki and Fitz-Simon in the autumn of 1966: 'I thought I was dying but I was actually pregnant! You don't know what's happening to you, I felt so bad. We'd been married for six years and Fitz was so worried about me he was going to take me away to Jamaica. We were in Paris at a hotel having dinner and I said, "I have to go outside quickly" and I just threw up all over the street and Fitz was like, Hello! We were so happy, Fitz was dancing all over the street.' The British couturier Victor Edelstein was working as a pattern cutter at Biba at the time and remembers 'Barbara being [at the workrooms] pregnant and looking terribly smart in the maternity dresses that she'd had made'.[21]

Witold Fitz-Simon was born on 19 June 1967, his impending arrival having already prompted a move to a house in Kensington's Brunswick Gardens. 'Fitz said, "I want the house full of flowers",' recalls Sarah Plunkett, who was godmother to Witold together with her cousin Rosie Marks, Hulanicki's PA, 'and I had to go and buy *masses* of them. I filled the house, all up the stairs in vases, for when she came home.'[22]

The family's new home was a dilapidated Edwardian building that, under Barbara Hulanicki's guidance, was transformed into what she described in an interview at the time as a house with 'a musty, cluttered look – a thirties feeling ... I can't wait for things to fade and

look old.'[23] Hulanicki created her new home using wallpapers by Julie Hodgess in the hallway and living room, and antique mirrors like those hanging in the changing rooms at Kensington Church Street (previous page). The same newspaper article asks 'What happens when a pacesetter goes home?' and shows Hulanicki sitting on the floor on one of her most prized possessions, an antique rug that had belonged to her father. Any pretence of a separation between home and work life had been given up, and the expanding concept of Biba was increasingly reflected in the changes to Hulanicki and Fitz-Simon's lives.

If this new house conformed to Hulanicki's vision, the clothes available for children did not: 'The clothes were so horrible at the time – rompers with three daisies on. It was so depressing.' Problems in life were merely opportunities for Biba, however, and the company's children's department was launched in 1967. As dictated

by the physical space available, it was not extensive. It was, however, revolutionary. 'We built a little house in Church Street at the end,' Hulanicki recalls, 'and everything was at children's eye level, at the child's height, so they could pick things, not the mother.' The twenty-first-century reader may take a more cynical view of the child as consumer but, in keeping with Biba tradition, the children's range was a logical step in offering every consumer the opportunity to dress as he or she wished.

Biba children's clothes were so unlike anything else on the market that outfits were regularly featured in newspapers and magazines. *Vogue* was one of the first,

Below, left: Child in argyle-print coat and wellingtons, *Sydney Daily Telegraph*, 22 February 1968

Below, right: Witold Fitz-Simon in Biba childrenswear, c.1968

Opposite: Biba childrenswear featured in 'Once Upon a Willow Tree', *Vogue* (July 1968). Photo: Morgan Rank.

with an outfit of 'Swirly colours of deep water blue and river bank sand, a coat cut with pockets flaring out over matching dress' (previous page).[24] This psychedelic-print cotton, an updated Art Nouveau design in acid colours, was a notable Biba signature look throughout 1967 and 1968 and was used for both adult and children's clothing (left and previous page). The bright and bold designs of psychedelia were pervasive in youth culture in the mid-to-late 1960s, filtering down to all manner of products, from home textiles and wallpapers through to ceramics and furniture, towards the end of the decade. Fashion was an early vehicle of the style, with high-street retailers and labels including Dollyrockers offering some of the first psychedelic-style fashions. In 1967, the singer Sandie Shaw wore a bright floral-print dress from the fashion company Bernshaw to collect an award at the Lyceum Ballroom in the Strand, London. The psychedelic prints at Biba were by Anthea Davies, a recent design graduate, who walked in off the street selling her designs. 'She came into the shop with this collection and we bought everything,' Hulanicki recalls. 'Her stuff was great, so we put her in a room to do the different colourways. Because it's one person that's designing them they all look slightly similar, a common identity, and the shop looked like an explosion of really bright colours. When Fitz saw it he was like, What?! I hope it sells.'

Biba customers knew what to expect from the company, with the most devoted literally waiting for each new delivery. 'On a Saturday morning [the customers] would be waiting for the delivery of something in particular that somebody had told them was coming in,' Hulanicki says. A hand-written order from the Biba archive, dated 6 October 1967, offers a glimpse into the range of clothing the shop offered. Dresses to be ordered include 'brown wool culotte (£4 19s 6d), check wool roll-neck (£5 5s), Zhivago in brown and grey (£4 19s 6d), mauve linen white collar (£3 10s), grey 'Ben Casey' (£4 19s 6d), mauve hippy (£4 4s), white gathered wool (£4 4s).' Hulanicki's working practice of creating new clothing designs almost daily (as opposed to designing distinct seasonal collections) meant that the style of particular Biba clothes evolved. '[Biba customers] just wanted mark I, then mark II and so on, you didn't need to

Jo Dingemans modelling 'psychedelic-gothic'-print dress, c.1967

Above: 'Biba of London renowned for their mini prices', *The Star*, Jamaica, 14 October 1967

Opposite: Barbara Hulanicki, assorted working drawings for catalogue illustrations, works on paper, 1969

small range of men's T-shirts at Church Street, primarily for Fitz-Simon's benefit.

The rapidly growing international reputation of Biba was given further impetus in August 1967, when the company was invited to participate in what Hulanicki and Fitz-Simon thought was going to be a small trade show in Brazil alongside established international couturiers. With the couple's son Witold barely a month old, it was left to pattern cutter Ann Behr and shop manager Eleanor Powell to attend in their place. They were joined by Jo Dingemans, a 17-year-old friend of Hulanicki's from Brighton who had been working as a model in Paris: 'The first night we got there we were at a reception and there [were André] Courrèges, Rudi Gernreich and Paco Rabanne. They were all terribly professional, with the Rudi Gernreich guys from [1966 French film satirizing fashion] *Qui êtes-vous, Polly Maggoo?* We really didn't know what we were doing [but] we were treated like superstars and we did fashion show after fashion show after fashion show.'[25] The media hoopla wafted across the Caribbean Sea, with a Jamaican newspaper issuing advice: 'Biba of London, renowned for their mini prices and skirts, doll clothes and stunning prints, are sending ... three designs to Brazil's annual fabric fair in São Paulo. The ladies of South America are warned that there is bound to be a minor revolution among the young generation.'[26] The organizers of the fair were so pleased with the Biba girls that they gave them a holiday in Rio de Janeiro. 'We went to the favela area,' Dingemans remembers, 'and slowly but surely there was this very big crowd [forming] around us. We had been having a lot of attention so we didn't think too much of it. Then they started throwing stones at us because our skirts were so short ... it was 1967, it was a Catholic country and we should have known better.'[27]

Without Hulanicki closely overseeing the running of the boutique, the Brighton Biba had lasted for just over a year. If Biba was to expand, it had to be done in a way that allowed her to control every detail, and so it was decided to re-launch the Biba catalogue (pp.96–105). 'Fitz thought it was the time to do them again because we were just growing and growing and he wanted to expand Biba,' Hulanicki recalls. She and Fitz-Simon had ceased production of an earlier photocopied catalogue (p.55) when the day-to-day running of the Kensington Church

reinvent the dress every few months,' she explains. Culottes and dresses with white collars had become Biba staples, their 'bread and butter', but with designs manufactured in such small numbers (no more than 500 of any style) it was also easy for Hulanicki to respond to the whims of the market, as, for example, with the 'Zhivago' dress (named after the 1965 film *Doctor Zhivago*). She also introduced a

Cotton Jersey cardigan set
No 4a — 4d.

1 Shier +
college scarf
2A — 2c.

Pirate Set.
No 7A.
No 7B
No 7C.

Corduroy Trench
coat + Skier
1A — 1b.

Polo dress +
Jerkin
3a — 3c

Neglisee + nightie
6A — 6c.

Hacking jacket set
No. 5A — 5f.

91

Street shop started to demand more of their time. The revived Biba catalogues would see Hulanicki working with some of the best photographers of the period and a number of her personal heroes, and would give her the first opportunity to create in photographic form the complete Biba look: 'It was just amazing to get it down on paper – it was the power, the absolute power over your image.' It was also an opportunity for Hulanicki to design a collection of clothing: in contrast to the continual development of design ideas she produced to stock the shop, the collections of between eight and 12 pieces featured in the new catalogues were designed to work as a whole and conformed to the seasons. Each collection represented the perfect expression of her design ideas at that moment, with the clothes designed to be sold exclusively through the catalogue, not as shop stock (although a few returned mail-order items would find themselves on the shop floor).

Designed by John McConnell, the catalogue was intended to appeal to the consumers' senses as well as meeting the practical concerns of the postal system. With its elongated dimensions (35.5 x 18 cm), the catalogue would slip effortlessly through a standard-size letter box, leaving the images unadulterated by any unnecessary bending by the postman. The Biba vision was delivered, perfect, to the homes of thousands of eager young customers. The catalogues carried the new 'Celtic knot' Biba logo (opposite), which has since become synonymous with the company's name, although the exact origins of the Art Nouveau-inspired swirl are unknown – McConnell based his design on a printer's mark he found in a book of typefaces. Hulanicki has since found examples of the same swirl in etched glass, decorating doorways dating from the late nineteenth century in the Polish town of Poznań. Whatever the swirl's origins, McConnell added the Biba name to it and, in so doing, created one of the most recognizable logos in British fashion history.[28] The Celtic knot design also appeared in printed and woven form on Biba clothes (p.121, left). Its use on textiles was aesthetically motivated, as the design made a beautiful repeat pattern for a variety of fabrics, but it was also a subtle yet effective form of advertising for the Biba label.

The first catalogue appeared in April 1968 (pp.96–7), with clothes modelled by ex-Biba shop girl Maddie Smith:

'I'd been politely sacked after falling asleep in the downstairs changing room while reading *The Brothers Karamazov*. I had come back in [to Biba] to show my friends the photographs I'd just had taken by Richard Dawkins, which I had in a little black portfolio, and Barbara got to hear about it, summoned me in and said, "Will you do my catalogue?"'[29] The photographer was Donald Silverstein, whose style – shooting his subjects from above, to create images of women with a large head and an attenuated body – perfectly suited the Biba Dolly look. The hair and make-up were an echo of the past. 'The ringlets in the front, that's my aunt's idea,' Hulanicki explains, referring to her reworking of the 'wigchief' (p.96, top). 'When she was in India on her honeymoon, because the heat was so sticky, she had these ringlets done on a band, which she could wear under her turban. So I did them in all colours – blues, purples, all sorts of colours – and they used to sell like mad.' The photographs were Hulanicki's fashion illustrations brought to life: 'Suddenly this thing appeared, this girl appeared in the photograph, and you're able to put all the elements together and it's really strong.'

Eight classic Biba outfits were included in the first catalogue, including a wrap-over coat dress (£4 19s 6d), a 'juggler-sleeved' blouse (£2 17s 6d) and a 'Battle Dress' (p.111, left) – a jacket with an Eton collar and a pleated skirt (£4 6s). Eschewing the more whimsical prints and designs available in the shop on Kensington Church Street, the catalogue presented a more timeless image of Biba, with the outfits chosen for their strong silhouettes and the quality of the fabric rather than any current ideal or fashionable print. Produced in crêpe, linen, towelling jersey and satin-weave rayon, the garments in the first catalogue were some of Hulanicki's favourites. The designs would be revisited and reinterpreted in different fabrics over the years – the pyjama-style lounge suit in 'navy, floppy satin', for example, reappeared as a short-sleeved pyjama set in printed crêpe, with a belt tied at the waist, in the last Biba store (p.192). A small selection of accessories to complement the outfits was also included on the back page of the catalogue. Adverts appeared in magazines such as *Honey*, *Petticoat* and *19* and in most of the daily British newspapers. The response was immediate and at times overwhelming.

As in the days of the Biba's Postal Boutique, production for catalogue orders proved challenging. Speaking about the re-launched Biba catalogues some years later, Fitz-Simon said: 'We had huge orders, but supplying them in a reasonable time was almost impossible because I, in common with everyone else, could not forecast the sales of an individual item. Every customer would complain on the same day that they had not received their order. In the end I had more people answering queries than I had making dresses. The finale came for me when a blouse that was one of several items on the page ... and of which only the collar and sleeve showed, sold 14,000 in the first week.'[30] Hulanicki remembers their friend Wally Rose, owner of the clothing company Dennis Day Ltd, being taken aback by the success of the blouse: 'He saw Fitz and said, "How many of these have you sold?! But it doesn't show!" He was in the real manufacturing trade and for him it all depended on the [descriptive quality of the] photograph in the catalogue.'

If the catalogue was designed to minimize damage in the post, the mail-order packaging was intended to dissuade customers from returning garments. Based on packaging designed for sending condoms through the post, the cardboard 'pillow' box created by John McConnell was boldly emblazoned with the Celtic-knot Biba logo in the Biba colours, black and gold. It was hoped that the striking packaging would eliminate frustrations if a customer received her order late, persuading her to keep the package and the Biba outfit. McConnell remembers the influence the Biba catalogues had on the industry as a whole: 'If you can believe it, there was an annual conference of [mostly male] catalogue organizers, and they held this first catalogue up and they all fell about laughing because it had broken every rule in the book, [saying] "This silly upstart moving in on our business has got it totally wrong." Within a few years the figures were phenomenal, and it changed the business totally.'[31]

Five more catalogues were produced over the course of the next 18 months. The photographer for the second (October 1968) and third (February 1969) catalogues was Hans Feurer, and the models were Vicki Wise, a Biba employee, and Stephanie Farrow, the sister of actress Mia Farrow, respectively. Helmut Newton shot the fourth catalogue (pp.104–5) in his studio in Paris and Harry Peccinotti, later the art director of *Nova*, photographed the fifth, which featured young Witold Fitz-Simon's nanny, Elizabeth Bjorn Neilson, as the model. (A sixth and final catalogue was shot in September 1969 by Sarah Moon.) The Newton and Peccinotti catalogues were, indirectly, disastrous for Biba, almost jeopardizing the future of the business. The two catalogues were released within only one month of each other, in May and June 1969, and both offered similar styles of clothing (although presented quite differently), including beachwear, printed cotton blouses and slinky hooded outfits. Production could not be managed and customers wouldn't wait: within a fortnight, thousands of letters were arriving at Biba enquiring about the whereabouts of orders. As the company lost time and increased manpower (for garment production and office administration), costs rose inexorably.

Biba was rescued by new business partners. 'We needed capital like mad,' Hulanicki recalls. 'We went to our bank and asked them to find us partners. They came up with Dorothy Perkins, because they were retailers too. The minute we had the capital we made them tons of money ... it was amazing, incredible.' Robin Napier, a director of the financial company Charterhouse Japhet, had arranged a business partnership for Biba with Charterhouse Japhet, Dorothy Perkins and Dennis Day Ltd. Dorothy Perkins, a nationwide retailer with nearly 300 stores, was run as a family business by Alan Farmer and his son Ian. Wally Rose, owner of Dennis Day Ltd, was an old friend of Hulanicki and Fitz-Simon's. The couple retained 25 per cent of the company, with Fitz-Simon as Managing Director and Hulanicki in complete creative control, and the remaining 75 per cent was shared between the new partners.

Revised Biba logo designed by John McConnell, 1968

93

Over the three years that Biba occupied the shop on Kensington Church Street, a new mood in mainstream fashion emerged. The Romantic look, a style inspired by historical forms of dress, stretched over the last years of the 1960s and into the '70s, exemplified by British designers such as Thea Porter, John Bates and Gina Fratini, and becoming synonymous with the company Laura Ashley. Historical references had informed Hulanicki's designs from the first, with large architectural 'Pugin' prints on cotton dresses and lace detailing on day and evening wear.

Hulanicki's approach to design had always been to combine contrasting design features into a single garment, creating new silhouettes relevant to the times. The Edwardian-style neck, influenced by images of Queen Alexandra, the wife of King Edward VII, was a staple Biba design until the end of the decade (pp.114–15). A lace dress from 1969 combines the high Edwardian neck with the voluminous sleeves of the early 1930s (p.115). The puffed sleeves of the 1810s appeared on ankle-length evening dresses (p.118) as well as on short dresses in Art Deco prints.

Construction elements were also taken from historical garments. In the orange 'Regency' dress (p.120), the bust is covered with a long length of fabric (which ties at the back to create the bow feature) – a design element similar to the bib-front dresses of the first decades of the nineteenth century. The Burgess Ledward print used for the orange dress is also reminiscent of the small monochrome floral prints popular in women's fashion during the Regency period.

The first truly 'historical' Biba garment Hulanicki designed dates from 1966 and combines design features from different periods: the high Edwardian neck, the large puff sleeves of the 1830s, the high waist and full skirt from the Regency era. (She took the Regency and Victorian influences from the illustrations of Arthur Rackham and Kate Greenaway.) The outfit, in white cotton (left and p.114), was intended for Audrey Hepburn as part of her wardrobe for the film *Two for the Road* (1967). 'So much pain went into that,' Hulanicki says. '[*Vogue* fashion editor] Lady Rendlesham came in and said, "I'm doing *Two for the Road*" and she asked me to design costumes for Audrey. I nearly had a heart attack with delight. I thought, I've achieved everything! It's too soon! And then I went to a party and there was John Bates and all these other designers and they were all doing Audrey Hepburn. I was so upset.'[32]

Hulanicki's dress did not appear in *Two for the Road* but Biba made appearances in a number of films over the

Gown perfect for Ball —or bed

by JENNIE DINGEMANS

THE origins of fashionable clothes are sometimes surprising. There are the obvious influences like a man's wardrobe and a child's, but the latest comes . . . from the linen cupboard.

The demurely beautiful nightgown in the picture on the left is made from two large sheets.

It was designed and made up by Barbara Hulanicki after she had fallen in love with the very old baby dresses sold in an antique shop in Kensington.

So, with her designing talent and the help of the linen cupboard, I can today show you a 1966 version of a Victorian christening robe that you can wear to a ball or to bed.

The yoke and wrists are smothered in old lace, the sleeves do up with little pearl buttons, and the dress with two bows—just like a baby's first nightie.

Jennie Dingemans, 'Gown Perfect for Ball – or bed', *Daily Express*, 20 June 1966

Kensington Church Street period. In *I'll Never Forget What's'isname*, an, ironically, now forgotten 1967 film by Michael Winner starring Oliver Reed, Orson Welles and Marianne Faithfull, the entire wardrobe of one of the lead characters comes from Biba (although the label is incorrectly listed as 'Biba's' in the credits). Carol White, of *Cathy Come Home* (1966) fame, plays a young secretary, Georgina Elben, who has an affair with Reed's character and introduces him to, among other things, the delights of Swinging London. Dressed head to toe in Biba, including outfits such as a pink chevron-print suit, a purple checked suit with matching hat, and a blue satin evening dress accessorized with a feather boa, she inevitably comes to an unfortunate end, dying in a dramatic car crash and ensuing fireball. The film even includes a scene set inside the Biba shop and shows the visual impact of Biba clothes, decor and people – a beacon in an otherwise drab world.

If *I'll Never Forget What's'isname* played out serious concerns regarding the merits of consumerism and women's sexual liberation, *Smashing Time* (1967) ridiculed the whole notion of Swinging London. The film's two lead characters, played by Rita Tushingham and Lynn Redgrave, move from the provinces to be at the centre of it all in London. Tushingham's character finds work in a boutique called Too Much, with windows painted-out in an Art Nouveau design and an interior featuring potted palms and Biba hats on painted bentwood hatstands. Biba had become the quintessential boutique: Swinging London incarnate, epitomizing newfound freedoms for young working women, for good or for ill.

By 1968 the offices and workrooms of Biba had been brought together under one roof with a move to premises in Old Court Place, across the road from the shop. Delisia Howard ('Del') joined the team in the

Stephen Fitz-Simon and Barbara Hulanicki in the Biba office, 19-21 Kensington Church Street, London, 22 August 1966. Photo: Eddie Waters.

Biba catalogue, April 1968. Photographer: Donald Silverstein. Model: Madeleine ('Maddie') Smith. (See details, pp.99–102)

Biba catalogue, October 1968. Photographer: Hans Feurer. Model: Vicki Wise. Dog: Hannibal.

Biba catalogue, February 1969. Photographer: Hans Feurer. Model: Stephanie Farrow. Hair: Cheveux.

OBSERVER

19 JANUARY 1969

Helmut Newton

EXCLUSIVE-HAUTE COUTURE BY MAIL ORDER

Also : America's new first lady talks to Kenneth Harris/The hell that was Anzio by Raleigh Trevelyan

Biba catalogue, May 1969. Photographer: Helmut Newton. Models: Donna Mitchell and Ingemari Johanson. Hair: Didier. (See details, pp.98, 103)

Biba catalogue, June 1969. Photographer: Harry Peccinotti. Model: Elizabeth Bjorn Neilson.

Biba catalogue, September 1969. Photographer: Sarah Moon. Models: Marie Knopka and Quinilla.

summer of that year and became 'the Biba body': 'There was an advert in the *Evening Standard* for a job at Biba. I thought, Great, I love the clothes. The shop completely knocked me out because I couldn't believe how cheap the clothes were and how beautiful the shop was, like a kind of oriental souk. While I was working at the shop they kept coming out saying, "We need a model to try the clothes on, size 10, who's a size 10?" Then Ann Behr, who was terribly aristocratic, came over and dragged me to Old Court Place. They kept measuring me and they said, "You're the absolutely perfect size 10" – all my proportions were right and everything.'[33] Howard stayed with Biba for the next seven years, and so invaluable was her 'perfect size 10' that Hulanicki had mannequin design company Adel Rootstein make casts of her and a number of 'bodies' for Barbara to work on when Del herself was indisposed: 'They're probably in some junk shop somewhere, living a very Biba life. I hope to find one one day.'[34]

The closer proximity of team members at Old Court Place encouraged greater efficiency and the exchange of ideas. It also resulted in some innovative approaches to office life: the crèche in Kensington Church Street was a logical solution for the young mothers at Biba, including Hulanicki, leading the lives of modern working women. Hulanicki also employed a dog walker to chaperone the growing number of dogs owned by staff. Biba became 'a family, a mad, dysfunctional family'. Julie Hodgess remembers a particularly difficult time: 'My mother came to London to stay with me and unfortunately had a dreadful haemorrhage and died in my bedsit. I had an appointment with Barbara the next day and I phoned her at 7.30 to say, "I can't do anything, my mother's here, she's died." Barbara was wonderful and on the worst day of my life, [she] and Fitz took over at the most devastatingly horrible time and made me feel so special and took care of me.'[35]

The last year at Kensington Church Street saw the next stage in Biba's evolution. In Hulanicki's constant search for new fabrics, she and Fitz-Simon regularly attended fabric fairs across Europe but always with an eye on cost – luxury fabrics were not within Biba's reach. The launch of a couture range in January 1969 allowed Hulanicki to work with leather, silk and fur, creating the Biba style for a high-end market. Liz Smith, a former Biba girl and now a journalist at the *Observer*, worked with Hulanicki on the launch of this new line. Smith wrote a cover story for one of the newspaper's colour supplements (opposite), with photographs shot by Helmut Newton: 'A week before the Paris couturiers launch their collections *The Observer Magazine* presents the newest name in British couture ... Biba.'[36] Five outfits constituted the first collection: a burnt orange dress in pure silk at 110 guineas, a vanilla-coloured caped leather coat for 120gns, a silver-and-gold sequinned dress for 100gns, a chocolate brown whipcord jacket and trousers for 60gns and a 'safari-style' jacket and jodhpurs (80gns) or skirt (75gns). As expected, all Biba outfits came with matching accessories. Innovatively, customers did not visit Biba for fittings as with traditional couture, but instead sent off for a form, designed by John McConnell, and added their measurements to a drawn figure. 'It is vital ... that you are measured accurately (get a competent person to do it for you),' advised Smith in her article.[37] Customers would be sent a toile in calico to make any final adjustments, with each garment then 'cut to individual measurements out of couture cloth with perfect buttonholes, hand sewn zips and linings of silk'.[38]

It was a bold move for the company, whose phenomenal growth had been in large part down to its mass availability, but experimentation and innovation had equally contributed to the success of the Biba name. It was for customers to decide whether Biba's next phase was a reflection of their own lives or a step into the unknown.

Liz Smith, 'Haute Couture By Mail Order', cover for fashion supplement to the *Observer Magazine*, 19 January 1969. Photo: Helmut Newton.

'Covered buttons were really important for Biba. It would all have been done by hand: the buttons made and sewn on to the garments – and that was for mail order!'

Opposite, left: Biba, gold sequinned dress, Britain, c.1967

Opposite, right: Biba, 'Victorian Gothic'-print cotton dress with collar, Britain, c.1968

Right: Biba, printed cotton bathing costume, Britain, c.1969

'The shoulders were always straight, very square. When you're drawing all the time you're into graphic shapes. You can do things to bodies with clothes – adding or taking bits here and there with some darts or little pads.'

Left: Biba, printed cotton dress with white buttons, Britain, c.1967

Opposite, left: Biba, printed cotton 'Battle Dress', Britain, c.1968

Opposite, right: Biba, psychedelic-print cotton skirt suit, Britain, 1967

'When I was visiting Australia in the 1980s,
all the manufacturers who'd copied Biba
clothes gave an amazing dinner for me and Fitz.
They'd all made a fortune out of the Biba dart.'

Opposite: Biba, 'Art Deco'-print rayon blouse, c.1968 (left) and Liberty-print flanesta blouse, Britain, c.1968 (right)

Right: Biba, 'psychedelic-gothic'-print cotton coat with Regency-style stand-up collar, Britain, c.1968

'You'd never get these lovely necks today. Manufacturers won't do necks like that now because people won't wear them – they just want to be comfortable.'

Opposite: Biba, white cotton dress designed for Audrey Hepburn in *Two for the Road*, Britain, 1966

Right: Biba, lace cotton dress, Britain, c.1969

Opposite, left: Biba, cotton velvet coat, Britain, c.1967

Opposite, right: Biba, cotton coat-dress, Britain, c.1967

Left and above: Biba, treated cotton mackintosh, Britain, 1967

'Mutton sleeves. My mummy used to wear mutton sleeves, so they remind me of her – she would have worn this.'

Right: Biba, cotton velvet dress with 1810s-style sleeve head, Britain, c.1968

Opposite, left: Biba, brown wool 'medieval-style' dress, Britain, c.1968

Opposite, right: Biba, printed quilted cotton trouser suit, Britain, c.1969

Left: Biba, printed cotton 'Regency' dress, Britain, c.1967

Opposite, left: Biba, 'logo'-lace cotton dress, Britain, c.1968

Opposite, right: Biba, 'banana'-print corduroy cotton dress, Britain, c.1969

120 Kensington
High Street

1969–1973

'You know what Biba reminds me of?' said one Biba bird, 'the couture – I mean the real, glamorous, old-fashioned couture – Vionnet and the early Chanel.'

Women's Wear Daily, 1969[1]

The final mail-order catalogue (pp.104–5) represented the beginning of a new Biba. Launched to coincide with the opening of the new Biba store on Kensington High Street, the last catalogue differed from its predecessors in subtle yet significant ways. The Biba logo, newly slim-lined and 'not so Disney' (right), graced the chocolate-brown cover and the images were shot on location, tellingly in the Brunswick Gardens home of Barbara Hulanicki and Stephen Fitz-Simon.

The models were no longer the pre-pubescent, almost genderless, girls of the first two catalogues but Biba women, with growing confidence and an obvious sexuality. Flesh was displayed in a seductive manner, through a see-through spider-lace suit and unbuttoned nightshirts. The photographer, Sarah Moon, created the most fully realized vision of Biba to date, succeeding in bringing the Biba stories to life – the disposability of fashion (models standing on old Biba catalogues), the nostalgia of the *fin de siècle*, and the glamour of 1930s Hollywood. The images display a new Biba girl, whose innocence has grown into confidence.

Moon had been recommended to Hulanicki by her friend and *Nova* journalist Molly Parkin, who had made hats for Biba in the early days. Moon was the perfect choice: her work contained strong narrative elements and she created drama through lighting and *mise-en-scène*, in the manner of the Biba shops themselves. She would become the in-house photographer for Biba's 'High Street' years, producing some of the most iconic images of Biba and of the period, including a poster catalogue for the press (opposite). Through Moon's work, the model and former girlfriend of composer John Barry, Ingrid Boulting, became the face of Biba. For countless Biba customers, Boulting was the epitome of Biba (p.132). For Hulanicki, she is the apogee of the Biba look, the vision brought to life: 'Ingrid was the perfect shape. The idea was that one was trying to get that shape on to people who weren't that shape. Long torso, flat chest,

Above: *Revised Biba logo designed by John McConnell, c.1969*

Opposite: Biba poster catalogue for the press, 1970 (details). Photos: Sarah Moon.

125

thin arms, low waist and straight hips. The silhouette was as long as possible, very childlike ... Like a drawing.'

If the final catalogue was a subtle extension of the Biba name, the new store was a radical departure. Located at 120 Kensington High Street, the building had become available in 1968 with the collapse of the Cyril Lord carpet company. The former carpet showroom offered more than 800 square metres of retail space, nine times that of the Kensington Church Street shop, and Hulanicki and Fitz-Simon set about acquiring the store and creating a new kind of Biba.

'Biba has moved into menswear, children's clothes, make-up, jewellery, cushions, carpets, paint, wallpapers, crockery, cutlery and a department store on Kensington High Street,' ran the newspaper advertisement for the Sarah Moon catalogue.[2] 'Rattan chairs, feathers, cushions, everything had a Biba look, so you could make a Biba room whether it was rust or black or green or pink,' says Biba shop girl Lilly Anderson. 'It was all those Biba colours people wanted, and it went right through everything – the make-up, the cushions, the wallpaper, the paint.'[3] The developing sophistication of the Biba Dolly was reflected in the growing sophistication of the Biba store. To celebrate the opening, a 10-page booklet known as the 'purple press pack' was produced for the media. The somewhat grandiloquent introduction explicitly acknowledges the transformation: 'On Saturday, September 13th 1969 the Biba Boutique in Kensington Church Street will close down. On Monday, September 15th 1969 the new Biba department store in Kensington High Street will open. The Biba department store will be Biba's first step into the world of the big store, and their final step out of the world of the darkened boutique ... Biba has grown up.'[4]

Each department of the shop on Kensington High Street was given a distinct look and feel. 'Everybody had their own uniform, which Barbara chose, so you knew where everybody worked,' recalls Anderson. 'The cosmetics girls always wore crêpe, so they'd have an outfit with a turban and make-up all in a single colour – one was in rust, one in blue, another black, with maybe four or five girls selling cosmetics. Household would have maybe trousers and a little top, like a T-shirt, and [for] the men's department [it] was a halter-neck, sequinned top and a satin skirt with a split up the side and a garter. You'd go in each morning and change into your uniform and do your make-up.'[5] The new or significantly expanded departments now offered Biba as a lifestyle. Department stores by their very nature had always been one-stop shops, but never before had a company attempted to sell life's necessities under the governance of just one label. 'It was always their

Left and above: Julie Hodgess, drawing for exterior of Biba, 120 Kensington High Street, London, tracing paper laid over photograph, c.1969

The cosmetics counter on the ground floor at Biba, 120 Kensington High Street, London, c.1970

ambition,' says Sarah Plunkett, who had joined Biba as the manager of the Abingdon Road shop. 'They wanted their own brand of everything and from Church Street they wanted to move up.'[6] It was only through their partnership with Dorothy Perkins that Hulanicki and Fitz-Simon were able to realize this expansion of Biba, and between 1969 and 1973, the company would be transformed from a London boutique into a label that was recognized, and sold, in 30 countries across three continents.

Julie Hodgess, the interior designer who had contributed wallpaper to the two previous Biba shops, remembers the derelict store before its renovation: 'I was taken to this awesome, monstrous great space which had been Cyril Lord Carpets by Barbara and Fitz, [who were saying] "Look at this, what can we do here?"'[7] The couple created

'We ripped out the whole Cyril Lord interior, which was a sort of Fifties modernist look.'

a very different Biba experience in this shop. Large, curving glass windows, based on an original Art Nouveau shopfront on Westbourne Grove, were added to the building, funnelling people into a large, open space, to be greeted by abundant displays of homeware: 'Satin sheets, fringed lampshades, lace tablecloths, gold-and-pearl-handled cutlery to eat with from gold-rimmed white china plates'.[8] In contrast to the two previous shops, the huge shop windows were not obscured by textiles or paint but offered clear views into the store. 'It was inside out, it was *there*, it had arrived,' recalls Lilly Anderson. 'It was much, much more sophisticated ... much more of a show piece.'[9] Window displays were eschewed, allowing uninterrupted views of the shop's interior, and gone was the black-and-white flooring, replaced with expensive, cream-coloured marble tiles. The walls were lined with dark wood reclaimed from the recently demolished St Paul's School in West Kensington, and a magnificent staircase led down to the lower floor (left). Victorian jardinières dotted the floors, combining the decorative with the practical: some were potted up with palms and others filled with sand for use as ashtrays.

Hulanicki was now designing a greatly increased range of clothing and product. Building on the success of childrenswear at Kensington Church Street, that department became much larger in size and range at the new shop. With a set designed by illustrator Malcolm Bird, the children's department became an Arthur Rackhamesque fantasy playground, with a giant tree in the centre and

Grand staircase from the ground floor at Biba, 120 Kensington High Street, London, c.1970

walls decorated with images of fairies. The clothes – miniature copies of adult Biba garments – hung from bentwood hatstands, displayed at children's eye level, as before.

The men's department was located in the basement, selling suits, shirts and trousers for the Biba man. The range wasn't a reflection of contemporary men's fashion, ostentatious and effeminate, but solid suits made for business rather than pleasure – although Hulanicki's initial designs did suggest a few features unique in menswear, as jackets with bust darts and sleeves that couldn't accommodate biceps found themselves momentarily in the workrooms. Biba clothes for women had also occasionally found themselves worn by men: a photograph of Keith Richards of the Rolling Stones shows him in the 'droopy coat in granny printed silky rayon' first seen in the fourth Biba catalogue (pp.104–5).

Cosmetics weren't reliant on body shape for appropriation and the years at Kensington High Street coincided with the rise of glam rock, the spirit of 'flaunt it if you've got it, and if you haven't got it fake it.'[10] Flaunting it were David Bowie, Marc Bolan and, most closely associated with Biba, Freddie Mercury. His then girlfriend, Biba receptionist Mary Austin, encouraged Mercury to experiment with (Biba) cosmetics and to cultivate a camp image, although it's unlikely Mercury needed much persuading.

As with the feather boas in Abingdon Road, the demarcation between Biba stock and Biba decor was non-existent. Two quintessential Biba homeware products were originally designed as decor for the Kensington High Street store but found their way on to the retail floor. The tasselled lampshades came in the Biba colours and countless sizes to suit any room. 'They were made to order, and you used to have to make phone calls to customers on Friday evening about their order,' Anderson explains. 'I remember phoning Led Zeppelin once, because Robert Plant had ordered some for his home, and being on the phone for about an hour as I was passed from one stoned person to the next.'[11] The 'lady lamps' in the Art Deco style – based on the 1925 original by Max Le Verrier, and cast by Nick Heywood in Westbourne Grove – also came to symbolize Biba from this period onwards.

The growing sophistication of Biba, both in terms of merchandise and retail space, did not go unnoticed by the media. Newspapers that had previously given the company only cursory coverage now fell over themselves to feature the new store. New York's *Women's Wear Daily* devoted a double-page to the shop, perfectly capturing the reborn Biba: 'The new Biba Department Store [sic] on Kensington High Street is the new mood of London … the first of the really hip, cheap little boutiques [has] gone the other way. Back to everything we think of as establishment and really passé. Back to dressing up for dinner in long, diaphranous [sic] dresses with hats feathered and veiled. To ball gowns in lace … to pink satin-on-the-bias negligees.'[12]

The Kensington High Street years brought to the fore one of the key Biba looks: the Hollywood vamp. Hulanicki had been designing 1930s-style, silky, satin-weave garments, redolent of the Golden Age of Hollywood, since Abingdon Road. The look had been worked and reworked through the Biba years and, with cosmetics now part of the Biba range, the ultimate 1930s Biba look could now be achieved (although the heavily made-up Biba look is arguably more typical of the film stars of the 1920s, such as Clara Bow and Theda Bara).

In complete contrast to the wide-eyed innocence of the Biba Dolly, the Biba Vamp was sexually alluring and slightly forbidding. Plunging necklines displayed her breasts, with garments in silky satins skimming the curves of her now fuller figure. The basic silhouette remained the same, with square shoulders, high armholes and a long torso; only the addition of curves acknowledged the Biba girl's development into a young woman.

The 'purple press pack' devoted a page to the improved couture range of Biba clothes, announcing that the 'Biba gallery will have elegant evening clothes in rich exotic fabrics, silks, fur coats, and fully lined trousers. They will be more expensive than the other Biba clothes – prices up to £50 – and only a very small number of each style will be made up.'[13] Launched in the last year at Church Street, the couture range becomes a whole department in Kensington High Street, occupying a separate space with an individual identity (opposite). The practice of sending toiles to customers and requiring them to make

Couture department at Biba, 120 Kensington High Street, London, 'The Boutiques Business', *Daily Telegraph Magazine* (17 July 1970). Photo: Brian Duffy.

adjustments was abandoned as part of a reassessment of customers' needs. 'They were beautiful clothes but you can't send a half-dress to somebody and ask them to pin themselves into it,' says couturier Victor Edelstein, who worked for Biba as a pattern cutter. 'You can go to a couture house, you can have two fittings with a professional fitter and at the end there will still be a little something that needs adjustment.'[14]

The couture range now reflected Biba's love of luxury and indulgence, with garments made of expensive fabrics. Located on the mezzanine gallery, the couture department was decorated in non-traditional Biba colours – 'all cream and pale decor, like a bedroom,' Hulanicki recalls – and assistants working in the 'posh department' would telephone down to the stockrooms if the required size wasn't available. Ostensibly about indulging the customer, this practice was in reality instigated by Fitz-Simon as a deterrent to would-be thieves, although it was not always successful. Jo Dingemans remembers selling a leather coat to Princess Soraya, the former wife of the Shah of Iran: 'I was so pleased with myself, but at the same time as me selling it, someone had managed to steal three of them without me noticing.'[15]

The couture range was not to last beyond 1971, a decision that had more to do with the public's perception of Biba than the quality of design and production. Biba was known internationally as a purveyor of fashion for all, and the elitism of couture garments with £50 price tags constituted a change the public wasn't prepared to accept. The mezzanine gallery was eventually given over to selling a range of slinky evening wear, which, in true Biba style, was labelled 'nightwear and negligees' by Fitz-Simon so as to be exempt from purchase tax.

Since the very early days of Biba, Barbara Hulanicki had wanted a cosmetics range: 'First you've got the dress, then the tights, then the shoes, then the hat and then you get to the face and … nothing.' Hulanicki's desire to create a cosmetics range perhaps went deeper than the wish to complete a 'look': 'I remember going to my aunt's on a Sunday wearing eye shadow, I must have been at art school, and she took one look and said, "Eye shadow should be a

shadow, it shouldn't be lighter, it should be darker." I learned something, I guess.' The Biba make-up range was indeed dark, and unlike anything else that was on the market at the time. Within two years of its launch, Biba make-up was sold in over 30 countries across three continents. Kolmar, a pharmaceutical company based in East Grinstead, became the manufacturer of Biba cosmetics after a rather unconventional introduction. One of Fitz-Simon's associates had found a briefcase in the back of a taxi, containing all the details of cosmetic companies and the formulation of their products. Fitz-Simon declined to buy the suitcase, but not before being made aware of the suitability of Kolmar cosmetics. The first meeting with the pharmaceutical company was, like so much in Biba's history, a struggle. 'We went down there and there were all these men sitting around, amused by us,' Hulanicki recalls. 'I said, "This is the colour lipstick that I would like" and they said, "Oh no, no, no we can't do that for you, it will never sell." So they drag the girls in from the lab to back them up and the girls love the colours – "Ahhh, yes, fantastic, this is so great. We'll do you a sample lot" – because they were so tired of mixing another coral or pinky whites.' In a 1973 interview with *Petticoat* magazine, Hulanicki said: 'People thought I was mad to bring out make-up when the market was already crowded. But it was crowded with twenty-five different pale blues and twenty-five pale pinks. There was nothing around to go with the kind of dirty, sludgy colours I was using.'[16]

The first batch of cosmetics, 60 lipsticks, arrived in one shade of brown and without any packaging. They were put in the shop and sold out within the hour. 'So then we were in the cosmetics business,' Hulanicki says. Delisia Howard, the 'Biba body' who now oversaw the cosmetics, also remembers this time: 'Loads of people said, "Don't sell the cosmetics cheaply because you won't sell them. People will think they're no good, and nobody in the cosmetics trade does cheap cosmetics." That isn't Biba's way, so Barbara went ahead and marked them up in the usual way and the rest, as they say, is history.'[17]

In another first on the British high street, people were allowed to try cosmetics before investing their money. 'In the beginning [customers] used to come in to the shop in the morning and they could do themselves up and nobody would bother them,' Hulanicki says. 'They would

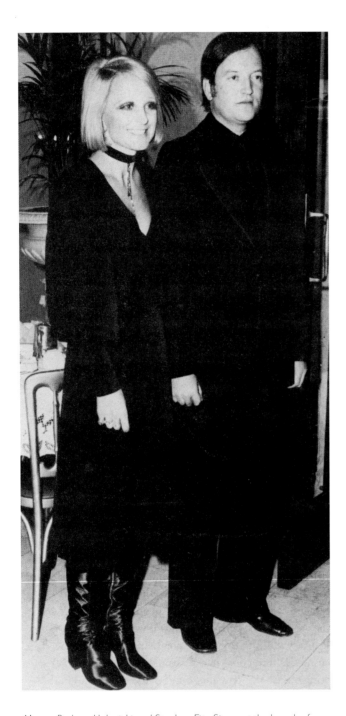

Above: Barbara Hulanicki and Stephen Fitz-Simon at the launch of Biba Cosmetics, Biba, 120 Kensington High Street, London, 1970

Opposite: Biba Cosmetics advertisement, c.1971. Photo: Sarah Moon.

come in, make-up and go to work. The corporates didn't like that kind of thing. They thought if you kerb it you make twice as much, but you don't.' The first cosmetics range was based on Hulanicki's early experiments with make-up at art school: 'The only available foundation in the Fifties was a stick, which was pancake and this disgusting colour, so I used to mix white gouache paint to make the colour I wanted. It's to do with drawing and illustration and colour. Our foundations were called "Yellow 1", "2" [and] "3" and they would turn pink on the skin. Conventional foundations were a pink colour that would match the skin, but would turn pinker on the skin.'

The partnership with Dorothy Perkins gave Biba outlets nationwide: the cosmetics were sold in nearly 300 Dorothy Perkins stores, displayed in small units specially designed by the Whitmore-Thomas design group. Within a year, the range was available internationally, through Galeries Lafayette in Paris, Fiorucci in Italy and Judy's in California.

The Biba face owed more to vampy Hollywood stars of the silent era than contemporary film stars of the day. It was an extreme look, with hollowed-out cheeks, dark lips and heavy eye shadow, all of which could be bought in a single colour palette: black, brown, blue or green. The effect was deliberately theatrical and worked beautifully within the dark confines of the Biba store. Venturing out in daylight was more problematic, as Hulanicki admits: 'I remember being in Milan with three of the girls and one had the complete blue look: blue lipstick, blue eye shadow, blue powder, blue eyelashes and blue wig. The other two had the same look with different colours, and they got in this cab on their way to Fiorucci and the cab driver almost had a heart attack.'

The success of Hulanicki's cosmetics is illustrated by the sales of false eyelashes. A big part of creating the Biba look, the eyelashes were launched as part of the cosmetics range and retailed at 65 pence. Not everyone approved of Biba's latest line, as a letter from the archive shows: 'Dear Madam, I must start with saying how disappointed I am that you have started to manufacture cosmetics, because at the moment it is very clear to me that you have a lot to learn.'[18] Sales, however, were phenomenal. Caterpillar and Spider lashes were introduced in April 1970 and, by early 1971, an order equating to 250,000 pairs was placed.

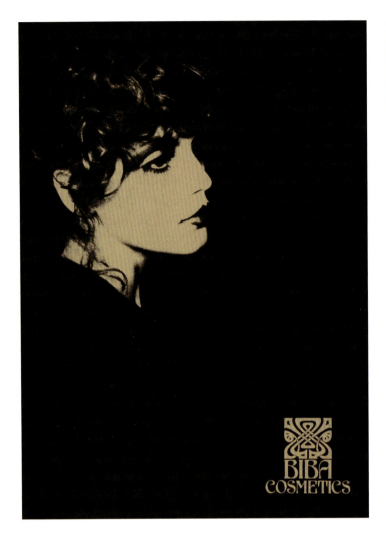

In August 1970, the first coloured lashes were produced, in four Biba shades – bilberry, prune, bluebottle and plum – and by June 1971, an order had been placed for 42,000 pairs in seven colours.

Seasonal ranges were also introduced, as correspondence from November 1971 indicates: 'The metallic ones are particularly urgent as ideally we would like them to tie in with a range of metallic cosmetic products we are doing in March of next year.'[19] An enquiry to Cardinelli Ltd, a manufacturer of false eyelashes, also asks whether 'the glue can stand up to water' for a 'beachwear' collection.[20]

Hulanicki was always one of the first to wear any new product, as she explained at the time: 'I always test every

Above, left: Biba Cosmetics advertisement with model Eva Molnar, c.1971. Photo: Barbara Hulanicki.

Above, right: Biba Cosmetics advertisement with model Ingrid Boulting, c.1970. Photo: Sarah Moon.

Opposite: Contact sheet showing Jo Dingemans modelling for a Biba Cosmetics photo shoot, c.1971. Photos: Barbara Hulanicki.

product which Biba produces on myself, as well as doing the normal tests that we run on every product before it's added to the Biba range. I want to know exactly how every product works at every stage of its development. I also like to see exactly what colours work with the clothes they are designed to match.'[21]

In 1969 Barbara Hulanicki designed what is unarguably Biba's most iconic product – the 'Biba boot' (below). Boots had been to the 1960s what stilettos were to the 1950s and Mary Janes to the 1920s. From Pierre Cardin to Courrèges to Mary Quant, boots completed the look of the 1960s, rising from ankle- to thigh-high as the decade progressed. So ubiquitous were they that fashion journalist Felicity Green was to able comically paraphrase Sir Walter Scott[22] and ask her readers: 'Breathes there a girl with soul so dead she doesn't own at least one pair of high boots.'[23]

Skirt lengths, and hence boot lengths, were on the move in the second half of the decade. The economic gloom that hung over the later years of the 1960s, resulting in the devaluation of the pound sterling in 1967, saw fabric manufacturers desperate for skirt lengths to drop for business to pick up. Designers, however, were not quite so ready to let the miniskirt go. 'Mary Quant has already said she likes short, short skirts. Barbara Hulanicki of Biba still loves mini-skirts but will be bringing out coats nine to ten inches above the ground to wear over mini-skirts and knee-high boots,' reported the *Daily Express*. 'No one length is "in" or "out" at present. It's entirely up to what the wearer thinks she looks best in. Perhaps the wisest thing manufacturers could do is to leave the hem undone – and let the customer decide for herself.'[24]

Stephen Fitz-Simon was adamant that Biba should cease selling footwear. Sizing issues with previous manufacturers had resulted in customers having to take shoes from two different pairs, effectively rendering one shoe from each pair obsolete. Hulanicki remembers her husband's reaction to her design: '"We're not doing shoes anymore, come and see what we've got in the back, all these left feet." But I just had to have these boots and we'd got as far as the sample. I could get as far as the sample without Fitz knowing about it, but then you have to order it and then you have to put the money down.' Hulanicki had her own way, and the subsequent success of the 'Biba boot' almost prompted Fitz-Simon to trademark the name. It was impossible to keep up with demand, with customers happy to take anything. 'The queue would be out the door, on to the High Street, so I'd go down and ask what colour people wanted,' Jo Dingemans recalls. 'I'd come back out and say, "Black, only black tonight" and nobody would move [from the queue], and I'd think, But you wanted pink!'[25]

Drapery and Fashion Weekly reported one customer's experience: 'Cat pushed, shoved and elbowed her way to the counter. Along with all the other boot hunters, she called out the colour and size required and hoped someone might hear her. Eventually the assistant produced one boot – you're not allowed to try on two at once. If one's okay, you return to the counter, collect its better half, and proceed to push your way to the cash desk. A great sense of achievement swept over Cat. Apart from the fact that she wanted size 3 in brown, and had landed up with size 4 in Oxblood, she reflected that she might easily have fallen for size 8 in any of the other shades. "Is it usually like this?" Cat sheepishly asked the girl at the cash desk. "It's usually much worse ..."'[26]

So successful were the boots that other retailers would

'Biba' boots, Britain, c.1969. V&A: T67A–1985.

conduct their market research in the dustbins of Biba, as Hulanicki explains: 'When the boxes of boots would arrive we'd put the empty boxes outside and then the shoe trade used to come and see how many boxes we sold and what colours.' The boots were produced for the next six years with slight changes in design – the length shifted from above the knee to below and the chunky 'Louis' heel was replaced by a higher, slimmer shape. A canvas version was produced in summer and Hulanicki designed a high-heeled 'fetish' version in homage to Pop artist Allen Jones. The price of the boots (£8 19s 6d) arguably played only a limited role in their phenomenal success; footwear company Sacha was producing a similar knee-high boot at a lower price of £7 7s. The significant factor was Hulanicki's 'matchy-matchy' philosophy, as journalist Jennie Peel points out: 'I don't think she meant to do it, but you'd have a purple dress so you had to have the purple boots to go with it. It was an ongoing look. Russell & Bromley boots didn't look the same as Biba boots with your Biba dress.'[27]

Above, left and right: Footwear department at Biba, 120 Kensington High Street, London, c.1971. Photo: Desmond O'Neill.

The success of the boot prompted the expansion of the footwear department in the Kensington High Street shop. Originally on the ground floor, the shoe department was relocated to a larger space downstairs, the design of which was a departure for Biba (above). The decadent feel of late Victorian and Art Nouveau interiors was superseded by the flash and glamour of the 1920s and '30s – a taste of the Biba to come, based on the luxurious Art Deco room the French actress and singer Mistinguett (1875–1956) occupied at L'Hôtel in 1920s Paris. Conceived by design studio Whitmore-Thomas, the footwear department also had fluorescent lighting, beckoning shoppers into the new retail space. 'It [was] meant to be like a stage set,' Hulanicki says. 'The idea was that that people looked at the shoes in the mirrored seats and they could look at themselves all over. Reflected back would be the whole Biba look.'

In the summer of 1970, the *Daily Telegraph Magazine* ran a story entitled 'The Boutiques Business: Their Owners, Their Clothes, Their Success'. Biba was on the cover, the Biba name and logo now the most recognizable of all the boutiques born of the 1960s. The cover photograph by Brian Duffy (opposite) shows Barbara Hulanicki and her young niece staring out through the 'Celtic knot' logo printed on the store's window. Two further images accompanying the article show Biba at its Kensington High Street best. Elizabeth Bjorn Neilson (the model for the fifth Biba catalogue) is shown on the shop's mirrored staircase (below), wearing a purple crêpe coat and trousers (15 guineas) with matching fitted cap. Hulanicki's niece also appears, wearing a similar outfit of a matching blue crêpe dress and cap at 6gns, with Hulanicki herself in a gold satin blouse and ankle-length tapestry waistcoat. In 1970, tapestry fabric was a popular Biba look, with textiles bought directly from traditional English manufacturer Sanderson. The floral-weave fabric appeared on coats and waistcoats in numerous colourways, including light greens, dark browns, black-and-white and polychrome (p.150). The *Telegraph* article also featured the boutiques Bus Stop, offering a Tricel suit for £8; Quorum, also producing crêpe outfits, with a minidress for 20gns and a long dress for £20; Marrian-McDonnell, with a jersey jumpsuit for 13-and-a-half gns; and Foale & Tuffin, with a printed cotton dress at £12 10s.

The continual expansion of Biba at Kensington High Street saw the label cross the Atlantic in 1970. Hulanicki and Fitz-Simon had made tentative forays into the American market while at Church Street, taking their catalogues to American manufacturers in the hope of replicating the success of the mail-order business there, but nothing substantial had resulted. By the late 1960s, Biba was available to a limited few in North America in an unofficial but flattering form: boutique owner and fledgling designer Norma Kamali had been buying Biba outfits on shopping trips to London (at retail prices) and reselling them to clued-up New Yorkers. Mass-market retail this was not.

When it came, Biba's official American debut was, by contrast, a carefully synchronized launch from three separate sources: American monthly magazine *Seventeen*, McCall's patterns and Macy's department store. Macy's were to sell Biba fabrics, which could then be made into Biba garments from McCall's patterns. *Seventeen* – a publication aimed at the teenage market which, then as now, had a circulation in the millions – would promote the whole enterprise with a fashion story for their January

Below: Elizabeth Bjorn Neilson on the staircase at Biba, 120 Kensington High Street, London, *Daily Telegraph Magazine* (17 July 1970). Photo: Brian Duffy.

Opposite: Biba photograph for cover feature 'The Boutiques Business', *Daily Telegraph Magazine* (17 July 1970). Photo: Brian Duffy.

1970 issue. This launch would bring the Biba style to every teenager in America, but without the responsibilities and headaches of manufacturing and retailing.

Hulancki and Fitz-Simon had become friendly with the journalist Rosemary McMurtney, who had worked with Mary Quant to bring her designs to America in the mid-1960s. They met at the Biba offices in Old Court Place: 'We just got on with her. We thought she was fabulous and we just became great friends.' McMurtney worked on the *Seventeen* fashion story, with Hulanicki creating the garments for another Sarah Moon shoot. Ingrid Boulting was one of the two models at the shoot, which took place at the top of the Parisian department store *Printemps*. 'There was this fantastic penthouse where all the directors used to have their sitting room,' Hulanicki recalls, 'and Sarah managed to get into these wonderful, amazing and fabulously huge rooms.'

The Biba fabrics themselves were produced by the British textile company Tootal and printed with designs originating both in-house and from the archives of Burgess Ledward. Available in Britain a few months before the American launch, they were then sold across America in Macy's (a specially designed portfolio folder contained samples of 15 different designs, in between four and seven colourways, available in both plain-weave and voile cotton). McCall's, a company that began selling paper patterns in the late nineteenth century, was by the 1970s one of America's biggest suppliers of sewing patterns. They produced four patterns that could be configured into 10 Biba garments for the promotion. For millions of American teenagers, the opportunity to buy Biba designs represented a tangible link with London fashion. 'I'd never realized it was going to be so big, but it was huge,' Hulanicki remembers. The launch for Macy's was a big story and nothing was left to chance. *Seventeen* created a 22-page, sepia-printed merchandizing kit for all participating Macy's stores, which included advice on the Biba boutique and its fashions: 'If it's soft … if it's flowing … if it's very, very feminine … it's Biba!' 'Princess Anne does. London dollies do. And so will you – once you see all the new beauties inspired by London's famous Biba Boutique

Photograph for Bergdorf Goodman Biba window display, c.1970. Photo: Barbara Hulanicki.

[sic],' a press release declared. There was also advice on special events: 'Throw a "Mad Tea Party" to give your customers the perfect scene to be seen in!'[28]

Rosemary McMurtney also introduced Hulanicki and Fitz-Simon to Colette Toohey, a young fashion buyer for the upmarket Bergdorf Goodman department store on Fifth Avenue in New York. Despite their initial scepticism, the couple were persuaded to open a Biba boutique in the store. Located on the sixth floor, the boutique was approximately the same size as the first Biba shop on Abingdon Road, and stocked lines from the London store that were felt to be appropriate for the East Coast market. With display units designed by Whitmore-Thomas, Biba 'banana' wallpaper, bentwood hatstands and potted palms, it was a piece of London transported across the Atlantic. Eight of Bergdorf Goodman's shop windows were given over to Biba, making these the first and only window displays Biba created for any of their retail outlets. This was also the first time that Hulanicki's photography was used commercially. Following in her father's footsteps, she had taken up the camera and, inspired by techniques used by the Biba catalogue photographers, sought to create the perfect Biba image. Used in window displays and promotional material, the resulting 'Bergdorf Goodman' photograph (opposite) was shot in Hulanicki's home in Brunswick Gardens. The model was Jo Dingemans. As an eight-year-old girl, Dingemans had been dragged into the ping-pong room of her home and dressed up so that Hulanicki could draw her and, as an adult, she was performing the same function in front of the camera: 'On a Saturday morning sometimes I would go in [to work] and there would be a note saying, "Barbara wants you at the house." I'd go to the house and she'd sit me down and put on my make-up and say, "Put that on, sit there." Of course I was free as well, which helped.'[29]

Bergdorf Biba opened in January 1971 to a rapturous reception: 'Biba bombs New York … For the first time in Bergdorf's history queues formed on Fifth Avenue before the store's doors opened … In three days they sold one-third of the merchandise intended to last until the end of March.'[30] Bergdorf Biba took $30,000 in its first week alone, and business was to continue successfully until 1973, when Biba left the Kensington High Street store.

As the 1960s were coming to a close, an article in the business section of the *Observer* summed up the 1960s

with a selection of the decade's 'movers and shakers', including Lord Stokes, the head of car company British Leyland, and Lew Grade, the media impresario.[31] The only woman to be included on the list was Barbara Hulanicki. Photographer Neil Libbert remembers the group photograph that accompanied the article: reluctant to take her place among the great and the good, Hulanicki didn't show up for the shoot and had to be photographed later and her picture added to the final image.

Hulanicki's contribution to fashion and fashion history was also acknowledged in the Victoria and Albert Museum's 1971 exhibition, *Fashion: An Anthology by Cecil Beaton*, which included a roll call of fashion greats, including the couturiers Cristóbal Balenciaga, Lucile, Charles James, Elsa Schiaparelli, Mariano Fortuny, Gabrielle 'Coco' Chanel, Jean Patou and Jeanne Paquin. The exhibition opened with the creator of couture in the 1860s, British designer Charles Frederick Worth, and closed with the latest London designers, who had emerged a century later. Taking their place alongside ensembles by Mary Quant, Bill Gibb, Jean Muir, Foale & Tuffin and John Bates, there stood Barbara Hulanicki's Biba outfits:

a 'black velvet day outfit' (opposite) consisting of 'a single-breasted jacket with flared back and a narrow ankle-length skirt worn with matching hat in French embossed velvet', and a young girl's dress 'with rounded neck and long flared sleeves ... ankle length ... worn with matching bonnets in French embossed velvet'.[32]

The two outfits and matching accessories that Biba donated to the exhibition (and which are now in the V&A's collection) speak of the timeless qualities of Hulanicki's designs. The early 1970s saw fashion designers producing clothes inspired by the Second World War, with Yves Saint Laurent's *Forties* collection from 1971 and the boxy, military designs of British designer Antony Price epitomizing this revival. The strong, square shoulder line of this era – a favoured Biba look – is not present in Hulanicki's donations to *Fashion: An Anthology*. The outfits are classic Biba, with tight, skinny sleeves, high armholes and a long torso. Her ensembles also expressed her attitude to fashion – the Biba philosophy – with a fully coordinating outfit and accessories: skirt, jacket, hat, jewellery. In his introduction to the exhibition catalogue, Beaton declares: 'Fashion is a mass phenomenon, but it feeds on the individual. The true representatives of fashion are often those whose surprising originality leads them to a very private outward expression of themselves.'[33] A more apt description of Biba would be hard to find.

Biba had succeeded in becoming more than a name associated solely with fashion. It was the purveyor of clothes for every occasion, of accessories for the individual and the home, and the focus of much attention, some of it unwanted. The bombing of Biba by the Angry Brigade, a British anarchist group, on May Day 1971 was supported, with unintended irony, by a slogan worthy of an advertising agency: 'If you're not busy being born you're busy buying' (paraphrasing Bob Dylan's lyric, 'If you're not busy being born you're busy dying'). Hoping to bring about a Marxist revolution, or at least advertise the possibility of one, the group's 'Communique 8' continued:

All the girls in the flash boutiques are made to dress the same and have the same make-up, representing the 1940s

Biba mannequin at Biba, 120 Kensington High Street, London, 1969. Photo: Lora Verner.

In fashion as in everything else, capitalism can only go backwards – they've nowhere to go – they're dead. The future is ours.
Life is so boring there is nothing to do except spend all our wages on the latest skirt or shirt.
Brothers and Sisters, what are your real desires?
Sit in the drugstore, look distant, empty, bored, drinking some tasteless coffee? Or perhaps BLOW IT UP OR BURN IT DOWN. The only thing you can do with modern slave-houses – called boutiques – IS WRECK THEM. You can't reform profit capitalism and inhumanity. Just kick it till it breaks.[34]

Hulanicki remembers the day clearly: 'I've never been so scared in my life. It was one of the only days that I'd managed to get Fitz out of the shop on a Saturday afternoon and we were going down to [antiques market] Antiquarius with Witold. Fitz called the shop to check everything was okay and Irene answers saying, "Everything's fine but this man keeps ringing to say he's planted a bomb!"' By the time Hulanicki and Fitz-Simon reached Kensington High Street, the shop had been cleared. The device went off, but no one was seriously injured. The Angry Brigade, in seeking maximum media exposure for their actions, had chosen their target well. Biba was rarely out of the papers, and epitomized 'boutique culture' and the rewards of personal enterprise. It was also one of the relatively few companies dominated and run by women. For Hulanicki, the bombing felt like a personal affront – an attack on her livelihood and her staff.

The Kensington High Street years were some of the most innovative for Biba, taking the company from a boutique with national name recognition to a label available internationally. The partnership with Dorothy Perkins had allowed Stephen Fitz-Simon and Barbara Hulanicki to create the most fully realized expression of Biba – one that extended the reach of the Biba name and satisfied customers and shareholders alike. The first 18 months at Kensington High Street saw Biba's ranges grow at an unprecedented rate. The last 18 months were even more frantic, but the results of this work would not be seen until September 1973.

In 1972, the Fitz-Simon family had moved to a new home, a one-storey house in Holland Park. The house

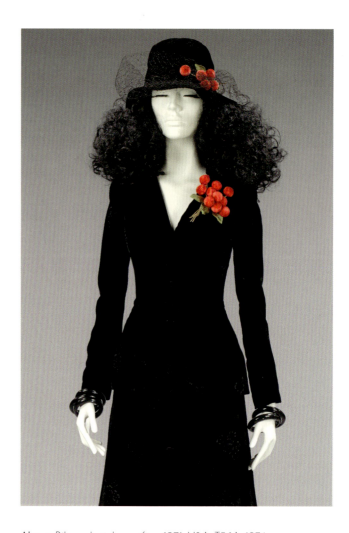

Above: Biba, velvet day outfit, c.1971. V&A: T56A–1974.

Overleaf: Interior of Barbara Hulanicki and Stephen Fitz-Simon's home, 1975. Photo: Manfredi Bellati.

was filled with Art Deco furniture, potted palm trees, textiles, ornamental trinkets, figurines and flowers (overleaf). 'Walls, ceiling, stairs, all painted a rich matt brown, merge into the shadowy interior; angles and lines are softened and blurred. Colours, not walls, mark out living areas, a different shade for each section of space,' reported *Vogue*. 'Everywhere, an endless intricate arrangement of colour, pattern, space; a deep, dark brown jungle of the ornamental, the exotic, the glittering.'[35] Their Holland Park home was a dry run for what was to be the ultimate Biba experience: Big Biba.

'We went to all
the fabric fairs:
Milan, Bologna,
Spain, Paris. I was
obsessed. I had to
see everything.'

Left: Biba, chrysanthemum-print two-piece satin polyester ensemble, Britain, c.1971

Opposite, left: Biba, printed wool dress, Britain, c.1969

Opposite, right: Biba, cotton lace dress with replica undergarment, Britain, c.1969

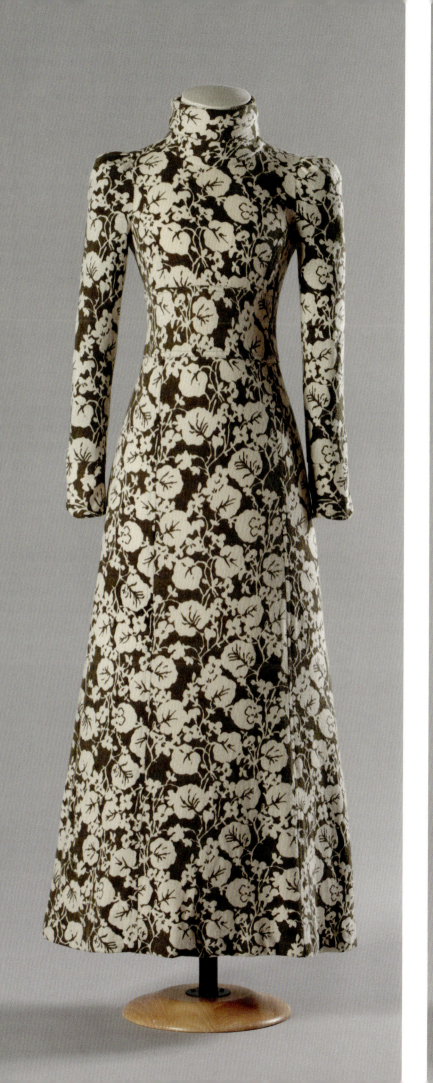

'There were a lot of military influences in Biba: these coats with frogging and high funnel collar, for example, and the "Battle Dress" jacket [p.111] from the first catalogue.'

'This was the
best print ever
– the little birds.
It just flew
out, on clothes,
accessories,
everything.'

Left: Biba, printed rayon dress, Britain, c.1971

Opposite, left: Biba, child's crêpe dress and cap,
Britain, c.1970

Opposite, right: Biba, crêpe maternity dress, Britain,
c.1970

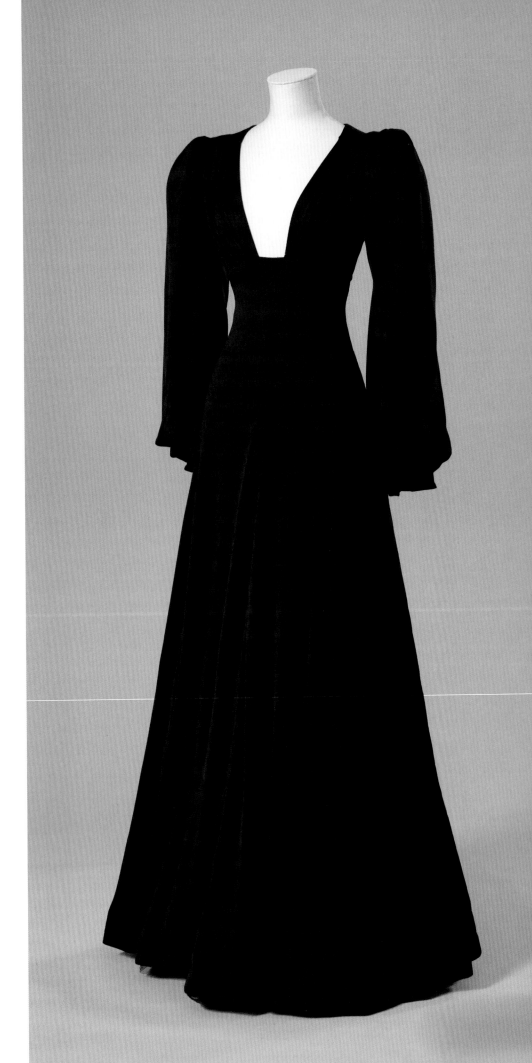

Right: Biba, black crêpe evening dress, Britain, c.1971

Opposite, left: Biba, black satin-weave polyester evening dress, Britain, c.1971

Opposite, right: Biba, couture crêpe and silk devoré dress, Britain, c.1971

Opposite, left: Biba, bargello-weave wool coat, Britain, c.1970

Opposite, right: Biba, lurex waistcoat, Britain, c.1970

Right: Biba, two-piece satin polyester wedding ensemble, Britain, c.1970

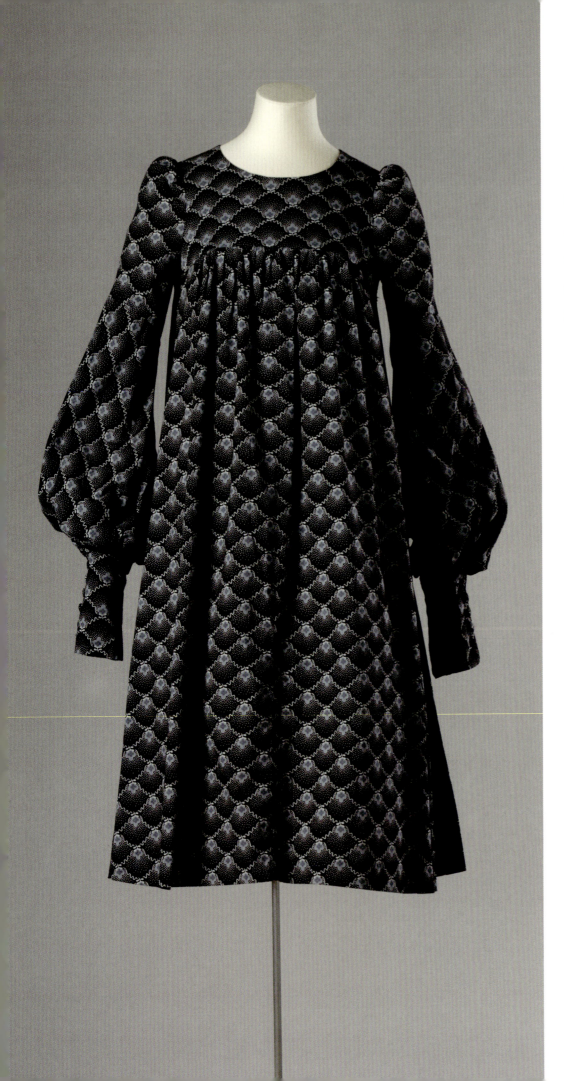

'The amount of
fabric in the
sleeves was huge,
and the cuffs –
they just got
bigger and bigger.'

Left: Biba, printed cotton smock, Britain, c.1971

Opposite, left: Biba, interlocking squares-print cotton dress, Britain, c.1970

Opposite, right: Biba, Art Deco-print dress with puff sleeves, Britain, c.1970

'Very graphic.
You know it
all comes from
drawing – it's nice
to do a drawing
with stripes.'

Left: Biba, knitted rayon and lurex evening coat, Britain, c.1970. V&A: T:202&A–1984. Given by Mrs A.C. Fraser.

Opposite, left and right: Biba, jersey dress (front and back views), Britain, 1970–1. V&A: T:120–2011. Given by Barbara Hulanicki.

Big Biba,
99–117 Kensington
High Street

1973–1975

'That scene at Biba's was very much like the Mercer Arts Center [in Greenwich Village, New York]. All these people got dressed up and came out and made a thing of it. It was like, we've got this costume, where are we gonna go in it?'

David Johansen, New York Dolls[1]

In 1972, Barbara Hulanicki was asked to design the costumes for a film adaptation of *The Great Gatsby*. Directed by Jack Clayton, the film was to star Robert Redford and Mia Farrow, with a screenplay by Francis Ford Coppola. Hulanicki was a canny choice – she had built her career on re-creating the past, but always with an understanding of the contemporary. 'I would have designed adaptations of the Twenties,' she said of the project at the time. 'Women just don't have that kind of figure anymore. They can't get away with the low-slung hip line and flattened boobs.'[2] It was a great professional and personal honour to be asked, but the job would have meant Hulanicki designing 500 outfits in two months, and six weeks on the film set, time Hulanicki could not afford to lose, and so, heartbroken, she turned it down (the costumes for the film were eventually designed by Theoni V. Aldredge and styled by Ralph Lauren). The start of 1972, however, saw Barbara Hulanicki and Stephen Fitz-Simon begin work on their

own Hollywood production, in which Hulanicki was responsible for costume, make-up, set design, catering and entertainment. Biba had bought the lease on the Derry & Toms department store on Kensington High Street in 1971 and, over 18 months, Hulanicki and Fitz-Simon turned it into a wonderland of escapism. *The Great Gatsby* (1974) went on to win a number of Oscars, including best costume design, but the latest incarnation of Biba would bring the couple international acclaim and herald a new form of retailing – shopping as a 'lifestyle'.

The behemoth of a building commanded an entire block of Kensington High Street and, with seven storeys, offered 18,500 square metres of retail space. Originally opened in 1932, the purpose-built department store was

Above: Biba logo designed by Whitmore-Thomas, c.1973

Opposite: Model wearing fun-fur outfit, Big Biba, London, *19* magazine (October 1973). Photo: John Bishop.

designed by Bernard George in the Art Deco style, with exterior ironwork by Walter Gilbert. When the store was put up for sale in 1971, the building's fate was uncertain. 'It was a ramshackle building which was potentially going to be torn down,' Hulanicki recalls, 'so Fitz rang up and we went up to the roof garden with Witold. I was in love with the building – all these incredible elevators and the surrounds of the lifts; it was so beautiful. I said, "Fitz, we've got to get this" and he said, "All right, I'll get it for you."'

Hulanicki had fallen in love with the Derry & Toms building back in 1969, when Biba was still located on Kensington Church Street, and she was determined to return it to the glamour of its halcyon days. Big Biba, as the new store was to be known, opened on 10 September 1973. Building on the success of Biba's earlier shop at 120 Kensington High Street, but in contrast to conventional department stores, its 15 departments offered customers the opportunity to buy almost any product for the home under one company's name (the only exception being electrical goods, which Big Biba never sold). The building also featured a one-and-a-half acre roof garden, the largest in Europe (a title it held until 2012). Transforming the interiors cost £1,365,000 (£14,000,000 in today's money) and Biba took temporary offices, which included a hairdresser's and a gym, on Harrow Road, from which to coordinate the operation. The internal transformation was achieved in collaboration with design company Whitmore-Thomas, with individual 'sets' built for each department.

'[Fitz said] he wanted it to open on 10 September 1973 – this was Christmas 1971 – and it did. He knew exactly what he wanted,' designer Steven Thomas remembers. 'We had about 18 months to design the lot; it was not only every single floor but it was also the graphics, the packaging, the design of the logos, typefaces, all the food packaging, probably five different matchboxes, four decks of cards, thousands of photographs and posters, even things like three Biba watches, Biba pens, Biba lighters, Biba address books, colouring books, diaries. The branding exercise alone for merchandise to sell in the logo shop was [an] absolutely extraordinary amount of work, which all had to be done by hand – the old, traditional manner – as we didn't use computers.'[3]

Whitmore-Thomas, working in conjunction with seven draughtsmen from Graysmark, a company that planned and built film sets (most notably for James Bond films), realized Hulanicki's vision of Big Biba in an array of styles: Pop art, Victoriana, Art Nouveau, Art Deco, and all with a nod to the kitsch end of Postmodernism. 'It would have been boring if the whole of Derry's was the same,'

Below, left and right: Postcard (front and back) directing Biba suppliers to the new store at 99–117 Kensington High Street, 1973

Opposite, above: Derelict interior of Derry & Toms department store, 99–117 Kensington High Street, London, c.1973

Opposite, below: Unknown artist for Markwell Associates Limited, drawing for the ground floor of Big Biba, London, mixed media, c.1973

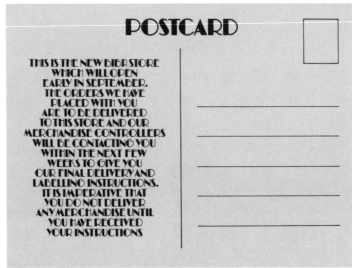

POSTCARD

THIS IS THE NEW BIBA STORE WHICH WILL OPEN EARLY IN SEPTEMBER. THE ORDERS WE HAVE PLACED WITH YOU ARE TO BE DELIVERED TO THIS STORE AND OUR MERCHANDISE CONTROLLERS WILL BE CONTACTING YOU WITHIN THE NEXT FEW WEEKS TO GIVE YOU OUR FINAL DELIVERY AND LABELLING INSTRUCTIONS. IT IS IMPERATIVE THAT YOU DO NOT DELIVER ANY MERCHANDISE UNTIL YOU HAVE RECEIVED YOUR INSTRUCTIONS

Hulanicki says. 'Each floor had a different carpet, from swatches we'd got from vintage shops, nothing to do with Derry's – apart from the Rainbow Room. That was taken from the original carpet and we had it made into a moquette.' The cosmetics department, with a cruciform floor plan, had display units based on the building's geometrical exterior ironwork (pp.182–3); the food hall was a Warholian, Pop art nightmare of giant baked bean cans and ring-pull sardine tins (right). The breathtaking Art Deco Rainbow Room at the top of the building (pp.172–3), 'in a class with such masterpieces as the Chrysler Building and Radio City Music Hall', was given back its coloured lighting and, with it, the justification for its name.[4] The apogee of artifice, Big Biba was the culmination of the eclectic Biba vision.

To celebrate Big Biba's launch, a Biba newspaper, complete with explanations of each of the departments and their locations, was printed and given away in the first week of opening. This playful approach, an inspired contrast to the high-minded and didactic booklet that had accompanied the opening of the previous store, was in itself a statement of intent. From a tiny boutique, Biba had grown to occupy seven storeys of prime London property and could afford to be witty, irreverent and ironic. As with the previous incarnations of Biba, the traditional rules of retailing were eschewed, the contemporary department store ripped up. Well-lit spaces were replaced with dark interiors, stock-laden retail floors were opened up into commercialized vistas, and sets created fantasies for visitors to inhabit.

The mock newspaper made for the opening was an unnecessary extravagance, as the conventional press couldn't get enough of the new shop, with the *Sunday Mirror* declaring Big Biba 'the most beautiful store in the world'.[5] Niche publications as diverse as *Glass Age*[6] and *Procurement*[7] featured stories on Big Biba in their pages, and newspapers ranging from Kensington's *Estate Times*[8] to the *Japan Times*[9] reported on its opening.

The fashion press was agog at the opulence and audacity of the store, and set fashion story after fashion story in its interiors. For its October 1973 issue, *19* magazine devoted its front cover and nine pages to Biba fashion (pp.165, 185, 187), and magazines in Italy, Germany, Sweden and the Netherlands also featured Biba fashion stories shot in the new Big Biba. British *Vogue* commissioned an article for

Opposite: Twiggy on the ground floor at Big Biba, London, *Vogue* (December 1973). Photo: Justin de Villeneuve.

Top: Food hall at Big Biba, London, c.1974. Photo: Tim Street-Porter.

Above: T-shirt counter at Big Biba, London, c.1974. Photo: Tim White.

their December 1973 issue, with the photographer Justin de Villeneuve showing Twiggy in Biba clothes in the distinctive setting of the new store (opposite and pp.171, 172–3). A whimsical take on *Alice in Wonderland*,

'Twiggy in Bibaland' shows readers 'what she found there: satin, sequins and a touch of art decodence [sic]' and invites them to '[step] into a Nickelodeon land of Art Deco – re-created by Barbara Hulanicki'.[10] Hulanicki designed outfits specifically for the shoot, with Twiggy in 'a midnight black satin long dress' in the Rainbow Room (overleaf), and a 'tight evening dress in satin with matching black edged coat' in the Mistresses Room. The photograph of Twiggy standing outside the Art Deco, Egyptian-influenced changing rooms shows her wearing possibly the most iconic of all Biba outfits, the 'great spot trenchcoat with hood over matching fake leopard pillbox hat' (right).[11] Looking back, Hulanicki says: 'I never thought at the time that what we were really doing were *the* images of the big store. I love them, but I never thought they would become the epitome of Big Biba.'

If there is one fashion motif that characterizes Big Biba's style, it is animal print – on clothes, homeware and interior design products. Fake fur had been a staple of Biba winterwear since Abingdon Road. Developed in the first half of the twentieth century, fake fur had been available for fashionable garments since the 1950s, but it wasn't until 1970 that a method was developed whereby to produce fake fur with non-geometric patterns. The early 1970s saw designers and retailers producing guilt-free 'animal fur' clothing, such as a leopard-print jacket at £28.50 by Brent Sherwood, a 'deep pile leopard fabric coat' by Martha Hill for £24 and a tiger 'skin' jacket for £26.50 by Scruffs.[12] With wide-leg giraffe-print trousers selling for £13.50, a leopard-print suit with a jacket and a skirt at £13 and £5 respectively, and a giraffe-print jacket at £18.35,

Below: Unknown artist for Markwell Associates Limited, drawing for entrance to changing rooms at Big Biba, London, work on paper, c.1973

Opposite: Twiggy outside the 'Egyptian' changing rooms at Big Biba, London, *Vogue* (December 1973). Photo: Justin de Villeneuve

Overleaf: Twiggy in the Rainbow Room, Big Biba, London, *Vogue* (December 1973). Photo: Justin de Villeneuve.

FIRST FLOOR.

CHANGING ROOM ENTRANCE.
LADIES DEPARTMENT.

'You could go for lunch in the Rainbow Room, or tea on the roof garden. You could spend a whole day in there. That's what they used to do in the Thirties.'

Biba was producing the look at the lowest prices and with some of the most successful designs: 'Biba, Britain's largest and trendiest Boutique [sic], is doing a roaring trade with a whole zooful of fake "furs" with all the gloss and glamour of the real, strokable [sic] thing,' reported the *Daily Express*. 'Other fur fakers have missed their aim by trying to make their fabrics feel "furry". Biba gets the bullet home first shot by focusing only on their tawny, glowing, photographic prints.'[13]

The glamour of Big Biba and the mood of the moment were a translation of the films of the 1930s, as personified by actress Marlene Dietrich. Theatre critic Kenneth Tynan once said of her, 'Dietrich has sex but no positive gender. Her masculinity appeals to women and her sexuality to men.'[14] Her films *Shanghai Express* (1932), *Blonde Venus* (1932) and *Destry Rides Again* (1939) originated the atmosphere that the new Biba hoped to express. Dietrich herself was very nearly Biba's opening attraction. 'She was going to come and do a residency at Biba for two weeks at the start, but eventually we got cold feet,' Hulanicki recalls. 'She was delighted to do it, she loved doing new projects, but she was going to charge us £30,000, on top of which we had to provide accommodation at the Dorchester [hotel], a white Rolls Royce, Joe Davis to do the lighting and, I seem to remember, two bottles of pink champagne per night for between her performances. We got frightened because we had [business] partners by then.' In preparation for the two-week residency, Hulanicki was invited by Dietrich's manager to visit the star's dressing room: 'She wasn't there, of course, but it was immaculate. Hardly anything there, just a lipstick and a table with that dress, that famous flesh-coloured diamanté dress just lying there, and a pair of shoes, very neat. Amazing.' If Marlene was the fantasy, Aunt Sophie was the reality for Hulanicki: 'That's what my aunt looked like. She would never have worn feathers or mink, because that was cheap. It had to be chinchilla, sable, fox.'

Big Biba was open from 9.30 a.m., closing at 8 p.m. from Monday to Friday and 5.30 p.m. on Saturday. The Rainbow Room remained open until 2.30 a.m. Monday to Saturday and was open on Sundays from 10 a.m. until midnight. 'You could go in there and not come out again for hours,' Hulanicki says of the store. 'You could go for lunch ... or tea on the roof garden. You could spend a whole day

in there. That's what they used to do in the Thirties; they'd come up from the provinces and have a makeover. But in Biba you didn't have to shop, you could just have a good time.' Biba offered an antidote to the austere mood of Britain in the early 1970s. Riven by economic problems and civil unrest – 1973 had begun with the three-day working week as a solution to energy shortages caused by the miners' strike – the country was in a 'state of emergency' and Biba provided glamour, decadence and escapism, all for the price of a bus fare.[15] Hollywood had landed on the British high street, and everyone could be the star of their own life, if only for a day.

The first floor, named the 'Biba Floor', was given over to the bedrock of Biba's success: women's fashion. Appropriately enough, it harked back to the company's beginnings, with Art Nouveau decor and the Celtic knot logo designed by John McConnell in 1966. 'All of the clothes can be colour-matched to different accessories – shoes, sweaters, cardigans, T-shirts, tights, bags, hats and flowers,' the Biba newspaper informed its readers.[16]

Art Deco prints were, by this time, a staple Biba look, appearing on vampish dresses with plunging necklines and billowing bishop sleeves in geometric form (p.193, left); on trouser suits with design features reminiscent of the 1930s, including Oxford bags and jackets with wide lapels (p.209, left); and on a two-piece consisting of a wrap-over top and a miniskirt. As with the first Biba trouser suit in pinstripe fabric, (pp.38–9) Hulanicki's use of these fabrics had personal associations. A photograph in the Biba archive in Miami shows her parents on their honeymoon: her mother wears a cardigan with an L-shaped Art Deco design in white on a black background, which Barbara had reproduced and used on a variety of Biba garments, including a skirt suit from 1973 (p.198, left).

David Bowie, Marc Bolan and Freddie Mercury (the boyfriend of Biba girl Mary Austin) were regular visitors to Biba, and it became the unofficial hub of the glam rock scene. Mercury described it as 'a beautiful shop done up well. When [Queen] fans come over here, that ought to be the first place they go.'[17] Glam rock reached its peak in 1974, with the fashions of that year shining their brightest before being extinguished by the coming recession.

Women at the bar in Big Biba, London, c.1974. Photo: Manfredi Bellati.

Hulanicki revisited her own design history with a Regency-inspired dress (p.196) that took its cue from Biba designs of 1967 and 1968 (p.120), updated in a black, blue and gold striped lamé. The classic Biba trouser suit was also given a glam makeover in cotton-backed satin, available in a range of shockingly bright colours (p.203), with matching hats also on sale.

The 1940s revival reached its peak at the same time as glam rock. The Forties silhouette, with its wide shoulders and boxy tailoring, inspired Hulanicki to produce some of the strongest Biba shapes of this period, including a woven wool coat (p.205); a matched outfit consisting of a striped coat, blouse and trousers; and, an unmistakable Biba garment, the redesigned Biba mackintosh (p.117), which had first appeared in the second Biba catalogue of 1968.

The first years of the 1970s also saw the growing influence of 1950s fashion. Mr Freedom, the clothing boutique run by designer 'Tommy' Roberts, sold bold, Pop art-inspired clothes in bright satins, beloved of pop stars including Elton John. Vivienne Westwood and Malcolm McLaren opened their first boutique, Let It Rock, in 1971, selling original 1950s records and reproduction clothing made by Westwood. Big Biba sold 1950s-style 'brothel creeper' shoes and bomber jackets (the jackets were unfortunately only made in children's sizes, p.206).

The spectacular 500-seat Rainbow Room at Big Biba was the focus of entertainment, operating as a restaurant during the day and as a music venue in the evenings. 'It was packed. We used to do 1,200 lunches every day,' Hulanicki says. 'We were the first department store to do French and Italian food, and we also had health food. We wanted really clean food, not awful stuff covered in sauce.' The first chef was almost constantly inebriated and unable to cook anything more complicated than a hamburger. Allan Gearing was hired as his replacement: 'I was living in Preston and answered an ad in *The Caterer* for the job. I'd never been there but knew about Biba – one of my girlfriends used to travel down to London to shop there. [Biba] was a crazy, beautiful place.'[18] As well as being responsible for running the restaurant by day, Gearing also hired bands to play at the Rainbow Room in the evenings. Bill Haley, the Ronettes and the Pointer Sisters all made appearances and even Elvis Presley, it was rumoured, wanted to play there. Most (in)famous were American rock band the New York Dolls (left). 'Oh, they were fantastic. They came up in the goods lift and they were very quiet, never said anything, very sweet and nice,' Hulanicki remembers. 'They looked amazing and so elegant, with beautiful shoes – sort of Jacqueline Onassis shoes, Italian shoes. I was so jealous!' The New York Dolls also made an appearance on *The Old Grey Whistle Test*, the music programme on BBC2. Bob Harris, the show's host, dismissed them as 'mock rock', an attitude perhaps

Left: Advertisement for the New York Dolls' appearance at Biba, *Gay News*, November 1973

Opposite: Performer on stage in the Rainbow Room, Big Biba, London, c.1973. Photo: James Wedge.

influenced by the band's outfits, which included Biba womenswear: singer David Johansen was in a black-and-white polka-dot blouse (a redesign of a blouse that appeared in the first photographic Biba catalogue, pp.96–7) and bassist Arthur Kane was wearing a black Biba jacket with leopard-print, fake fur collar and cuffs.

After the affected effeminacy of the New York Dolls, Liberace brought the genuine article to the Rainbow Room. 'It was a private event and the elevator breaks down,' Hulanicki recalls. 'It stops with just Liberace's head showing and I thought, Who's that behind [him]? Andrew Logan and Zandra Rhodes were gatecrashing. Of course, they looked far more exotic than he did. Liberace had on a double-breasted white mink with

diamond buttons, which he never took off. The day before, I sent Del [Delisia Howard] out to Sotheby's to rent a fabulous candelabra and it was worth something like £30,000. I said to Joyce behind the desk, "Whatever you do, do not give it to him."'

The Biba children's department, located on the second floor, now provided, 'everything for babies, children, "Lolitas" and pregnant mums.'[19] The Disney-esque sets included a Wild West saloon, a general store and a castle, as well as a bookshop with a Peter Rabbit theme and a children's eating area, complete with toadstool tables and seats. Babies were catered for with prams, high chairs, baby baths, beakers, spoons, dishes, talcum powder, cream and oils. Polo-necked sweaters in Biba colours were available for babies up to six months old, complete with matching tights, as were terry towelling nappies in classic Biba colours such as black, purple and dark brown. Children aged two to nine were able to emulate their parents, with a choice of outfits similar to those in the adult range that included 'lurex tights and sweaters, long black crêpe dresses for girls, satin shirts for boys; silver sparkly wellington boots, polka dot bar shoes and lurex baby shoes'.[20] The *Daily Express* remarked on this empowerment of children as consumers: '"These days, kids don't want to look like kids," argues [Biba], which sells a leopard-print christening robe to babes in the trendiest arms. "They have minds of their own. At three, they come in to us and choose everything, even their hats. They know what they want."'[21] The provocatively titled 'Lolita' department provided clothing for the Biba girls of the next generation, offering a 'leopard-print trouser suit and hat ... floral printed dress and matching hat ... green satin trouser suit and green feather boas', all scaled-down versions of adult garments (left).[22]

The men's clothing on offer had evolved from the T-shirts on sale at Kensington Church Street to complete outfits, including the necessary accoutrements of a gentleman – monocles and silver-topped canes. The entire third floor was given over to this department, which now

Left: Outfits from the 'Lolita' and adult departments, *Country Life* (27 December 1973). Photo: Christopher Moore.

Opposite: Men's shoe display at Big Biba, London, 1974. Photo: Tim Street-Porter.

also included boys' clothing. It was fitted out in dark wood with dusky, sombre carpets and glass-fronted walnut cabinets – the only original item of shop furniture retained from the 1930s interior of Derry & Toms.

In contrast to the women's clothing, the men's range was, on the whole, a rather muted affair, but, in true Biba style, harked back to a classic age of men's tailoring – a time when Hulanicki's father was still alive. A large-check, double-breasted, three-piece wool suit (p.208), with broad shoulders and wide lapels, is redolent of the 1930s and the suits produced by the British manufacturer Montague Burton (a company which, it has been estimated, dressed one fifth of the male population of Britain in the 1930s), or the suits favoured by film stars of the period, such as Edward G. Robinson. Not all the suits were as unassuming, with a number described as having 'an exaggerated all but feminine look about them' by the *Evening Standard*: 'Their high-padded shoulders must be the highest in town,' the newspaper declared.[23] A surviving fake fur coat (p.195) also belies a less conservative approach in Biba menswear.

In a 1974 article entitled 'What fits Fitz, fits Biba', Hulanicki discussed the company's menswear: '[I said,] "the philosophy is that Fitz has to wear the clothes", to which Fitz replied, "and if you're not my size you've had it!" We have tried to stick to the middle of the road [because] we have found that conventional clothes sell best and out of, say, 24 colours of an item, it is always the safe, sombre colours that go. Black sells so quickly it usually looks as if we don't stock it. Now we use bright colours to jazz up the place.'

Fitz-Simon's understanding of the power of the Biba name led to the creation of the logo shop on the ground floor, which sold assorted memorabilia, from playing cards and matches to postcards and colouring books. For the price of 10 pence, the logo shop allowed even those of meagre means to buy a badge and become a player in the Biba world: 'Consequently, it was one of the busiest counters in the whole store. It was also the smallest.'[24]

The constraints of time and economics meant that not all of Big Biba's vast retail space opened in September 1973. New departments were to open over the course of 1974, extending the range and vision of Biba even further. The roof garden reopened in May 1974, after the replanting

of the three separate areas: the English Woodland and the Spanish and Tudor gardens. Sculptor Andrew Logan added sculptures of a red rose, a white oriental lily and a black hellebore, each one three metres high and appearing both as if planted in herbaceous borders and as stand-alone sculptures.

Originally opened in 1938, with a tea pavilion and terrace, the roof garden had seen famous guests including film stars John Gielgud and Leslie Howard, and royalty from Britain, Norway and the Netherlands, visiting in the pre-war period. Its latest incarnation was no less glamorous. The reopening – 'a Gatsby extravaganza' – featured entertainment from fire-eaters, belly dancers, a tight-rope walker and a strong man, and, according to journalist and professional socialite Sandy Fawkes, some exotic guests: 'A cadaverous girl baring one skeletal shoulder haunted the terrace ... [and] two fellas – one in red, one in pink – both wearing make-up and discussing how you have to suffer for beauty'.[25] Fawkes also reported the attendance of some Biba stalwarts: Andrew Logan, artist Patrick Hughes, Zandra Rhodes, Ossie Clark and the actor Rodney Bewes (who was now married to a Biba girl, Daphne Bewes). The photographer Mick Rock also remembers these events: '[Biba] had these big parties on the roof garden or in the Rainbow Room, and you'd see everybody there: Justin de Villeneuve, Michael Roberts, Janet Street-Porter, Amanda Lear, Freddie Burretti, Molly Parkin, Andrew Logan, Derek Jarman ... and everyone bought their clothes at Biba.'[26]

The Biba Beauty Parlour opened in September 1974 (overleaf). Designed by Whitmore-Thomas, it kept to the original layout and details of Derry & Toms' beauty parlour, with a curvilinear, monochrome interior that harked back to the 1930s Hollywood make-up studios of Max Factor and Helena Rubinstein. Within the fashion industry, make-up artists were a relatively new phenomenon and it wasn't considered mandatory in the early 1970s to have a make-up artist at editorial fashion shoots. The opportunity for people on the street to get advice on cosmetics, or a makeover, was a revolution and, for some, a revelation: 'I learnt more

Opposite: Barbara Hulanicki in the roof garden of Big Biba, London, c.1974. Photo: Desmond O'Neill.

Overleaf: Big Biba cosmetics displays, London, c.1973. Photo: Tim White.

in one half-hour ... than I have done in all the years I have been using make-up,' said one satisfied customer.[27]

In a 1974 newspaper article entitled 'Hello Hollywood', Hulanicki said: 'We've been wanting to do this [beauty parlour] for a long time. But we've only recently found the person to do it.'[28] The person they'd found was Regis Huet, one of the first make-up artists to work in the fashion industry, who would go on to work with all the major cosmetic houses, including Yves Saint Laurent, Chanel and Lancôme. For the price of £10, Huet would 'transform your hair and make-up' and, for half that fee, he gave advice on cosmetics and suitable colours.[29] The beauty parlour was aimed at visiting celebrities looking for 'really special looks' or 'our average girl shopper coming in once a month for a totally new image.'[30]

New cosmetics were now introduced at seasonal intervals, designed to match the colours of the clothes. 'There would be the basic colours and then you would bring out capsule collections – in summer, you'd bring out pale colours,' Hulanicki explains. 'China Doll was [a range of] foundations and then you'd have ranges like Pop, which would [be] in and out. The ranges just grew and grew and grew.' The physical retail space for cosmetics had been significantly increased, with the aim of avoiding the scenes at the Kensington High Street store, with people 'ten-deep trying to buy cosmetics'.[31] The cosmetics range was now the most lucrative department of the company, turning a profit in excess of £600,000. 'Biba is to double its sales in Japan,' The Director reported in 1974. '[This] will bring turnover of Biba cosmetics in Japan up to nearly £1m in the coming year.'[32]

Big Biba was the first British high-street retailer to sell a range of cosmetics for black skin – other companies such as Outdoor Girl produced ranges for black and darker skin, such as the Tawny range (which came in four shades, from light to very dark), but they were not high-street retailers. 'In Abingdon Road there was only one black girl that used to come in, the actress Glenna Forster-Jones – she was so beautiful,' Hulanicki recalls. 'Then in the big store, there were suddenly all these black girls coming in and working in there. I thought, Wow, let's do a cosmetic range, so we did all the foundations. I think there were four or five colours, only foundations and powders, as the other Biba cosmetic colours looked fabulous [on black

skin].' Men also got their own cosmetics range, with the Evening Standard reporting, 'There will be a special range of make-up for men, the first of its sort ever.' Mary Quant had in fact produced a make-up box for men, but it was not what could be considered a 'range'. 'Not another range of colognes and aftershaves,' the Standard continued, 'this one will be something new, probably trend setting too. "We are preparing a big range of face things like powder, tinted pencils, light and dark foundations and painty things like mascaras," [Hulanicki] explains. "As soon as the packaging is right they will be on sale in the men's department."'[33]

There were also plans to open a cinema, which would have taken the Biba vision full circle, bringing to life the film stars who had originally inspired the Biba look. It was unfortunately not to be, as issues with licencing the films meant the project never got off the ground. Plans for a designers' market were also never realized: Fitz-Simon's proposal to lease half the remaining unused retail space, almost 4,000 square metres, to designers and antique stalls complementing the Biba style was not given the go-ahead by their partners.

With 15 departments spread over six floors, the sheer size of Big Biba had its advantages and disadvantages. The building could accommodate every department in a single space, with Fitz located on the top floor, 'in an office large enough to make the billiard's table it contains look like a coffee table,' as it was described in an interview at the time.[34] Hulanicki's own open-plan office meanwhile was the creative hub of Biba. At one end was Ann Behr, with pattern cutters and machinists making the first samples and production patterns. The art department, based at a large desk to Hulanicki's right, oversaw the colourways for prints, and Delisia Howard worked on cosmetics at a desk adjacent to assistants working on jumpers, bags, shoes and fabrics. The office arrangement allowed for immediate exchange between design and production: 'Fitz would come down and say, "Okay, how many patterns are ready? What state are they in? Are they graded?"' He was one of the first high street retailers to

Mouche wearing matching lurex jacket and pillbox hat ensemble, seated in the reception area of the Rainbow Room at Big Biba, London, 19 magazine (October 1973). Photo: John Bishop.

use computers to calculate fabric lays, minimizing fabric waste and keeping costs to the absolute minimum. Innovations from Old Court Place, the previous work-rooms and offices located opposite the shop on Kensington Church Street, were also carried over to Big Biba. 'On the second floor, there was a big crèche where the girls could bring their babies,' Hulanicki explains. 'There was a nurse, [who] they employed, but we gave them things like fridges, cookers and tables.'

The store's size necessitated a stockroom on each floor, and nothing went on display without Hulanicki's personal approval. 'Everything that came in the store from manufacturers would be placed on a trestle table in the stockroom with a piece of paper underneath it with its style number. Barbara would then go round and either sign it off or not and only those which had been signed for were allowed on the shop floor,' remembers Lorraine Harper. 'Barbara was creating the design, Barbara was designing the fabric, Barbara was deciding all the trimmings' so Harper had been employed in the previous store to oversee cut, make and trim (CMT).[35]

Working across seven floors also took its toll physically, as Hulanicki recalls: 'There were no cell phones, no computer, so you had to walk to people's offices, and we made a rule that no member of staff would use the lifts, as they were for the customers. In order to talk to somebody, you might get lucky in the stockroom or the internal phone, but it was exhausting and no one was used to it.'

Shoplifting also increased in line with the size of the store, although Big Biba was never the thieves' paradise it was commonly believed to be. 'We managed to keep the direct theft to around 2% of turnover, as opposed to a multiple's store's target of 1%,' Fitz-Simon once noted.[36] Biba's policy of always prosecuting thieves was, in the more serious cases, reported in the media, skewing perception of the extent of the problem.

Barbara Hulanicki's decade-long career in fashion design was a process of experimentation and Big Biba was the culmination of all those lessons: 'We got better and better and better over the years. It was like learning to drive and you'd suddenly realize, Oh, now we can do this, now we can do that. That's why it was so amazing in the big store because it was like a smoothly running engine. It was incredible, wonderful.'

The photograph of the almost completely naked model Mouche sprawled across Biba cushions (overleaf) has become one of the iconic Biba images. Her nakedness, advertising what was ostensibly a clothing store, is without irony – Biba was no longer solely a fashion company, but a name recognized across four continents as a retail phenomenon. Its diversification into every conceivable product was a symptom of its success rather than the reason for it: Biba had, in just a decade, transcended its origins as a small boutique selling a small selection of dresses. This particular image was shot in Hulanicki's home by her old friend and boutique 'rival' James Wedge, who had taken up photography in the late 1960s. He was commissioned by Hulanicki to take a picture for a rare – and unusual – Biba advert. 'It was going to be a 48-sheet poster, a huge size, which was going to be used at Heathrow as you drove out, and underneath [the poster] was going to be written, "Welcome to Biba",' Wedge remembers. 'Fitz called me and said, "It's been banned", so [Biba] did them as posters and sold them in the shop.'[37]

For Hulanicki, two garments capture the essence of Biba and represent the pinnacle of the company's design and manufacturing: a black crêpe evening dress from 1973 (p.197, right and opposite) and a purple linen day suit from 1974 (p.200, left). The crêpe 'Vargas' dress – inspired by a pin-up girl painted by Alberto Vargas – is more complex in design and more detailed than other Biba garments from the period, with a very low bust line and wide shoulders, a lined peplum in two sections and an integral pocket. The 'Vargas' required dozens of samples and it was two years in production before the design was finally realized. This relentless pursuit of perfection set Hulanicki apart on the high street and her ethic was fundamental to the success of the Biba label. The linen day suit epitomizes the ideal Biba style: tight-fitting with a long torso, high armholes and wide shoulders, in the quintessential Biba colour, purple. 'It's fabulous,' Hulanicki says. 'This jacket gives you a really long silhouette and those shoulders a really strong shape, like a drawing, an illustration.'

Opposite: Mouche modelling the 'Vargas' dress in the Rainbow Room at Big Biba, London, *19* magazine (October 1973). Photo: John Bishop.

Overleaf: Mouche nude, c.1974. Photo: James Wedge.

'I was okay for two days and then it hit me. I didn't know who I was any more. Biba had been my life, my dream.'[38]

The end of Biba was to be as spectacular as its rise, with the company faltering and falling within the space of nine short months. Although no one could have predicted as much, 1974 was to be the last year that Biba was running at full strength: a well-oiled machine that, over the previous decade, had built up a reliable source of manufacturers and suppliers, staff that understood the Biba vision and customers who trusted the name. By Christmas of that year, the wheels had fallen off. The business partnership Hulanicki and Fitz-Simon had signed in 1969 with the family who owned Dorothy Perkins underwent a fundamental change in the summer of 1973. British Land, a property investment company, acquired Dorothy Perkins for its considerable property portfolio and thus became the owners of Biba. Having survived Britain's economic and political problems in the first half of the 1970s, the high inflation rates and ensuing crash in the property market signalled the end for Hulanicki and Fitz-Simon's Biba. On learning of British Land's acquisition, Fitz-Simon said to his wife, 'You do know that's the end of us, don't you?'

Biba was the leaseholder of one of the most desirable properties on British Land's books – a building and a plot of land with huge financial potential. 'It wasn't personal, it wasn't about Biba, it could have been anybody in there,' Hulanicki says. 'They just wanted the building. The building was worth more to them than having us in there.'

The new owners of Biba installed their own team of managers, intent on re-creating Biba using well-established retail practices. The unique Biba display cases were replaced with standard shelving, which offered no additional display space. Big Biba also gained window displays, strip lighting and signs directing customers to the renamed departments, which included the 'Groovy Food Hall' and 'Junior Miss' (formerly 'Lolita'). As business evaporated, departments were 'rationalized', with the men's departments on the third floor closing down and relocating to the ground floor in February 1975. As Hulanicki and Fitz-Simon fought to save their company, design and production ground to a halt and, with a withering supply of stock, further departments closed. There was even a rumour that the building might be knocked down, although the couple had had a preservation order put on it: 'Freddie Mercury had told us to do it while planning a funeral for Biba, with horses going down High Street Kensington. Good old Freddie saves Derry & Toms.' Eventually banned from talking to the members of staff she had employed, Barbara Hulanicki left the company she had created in the summer of 1975, after realizing that she and her husband had lost control. Biba was, by this point, a company she no longer recognized and, understanding it was over, she walked away.

Barbara Hulanicki wearing a fun-fur coat, 1974. Photo: Mick Rock.

'We were always
desperate
for something
different.
We'd always
have hundreds
of fabric reps
coming into Biba
and we produced
thousands of
in-house prints.'

Left: Biba, cherry-print marocain lounge pyjamas, Britain, c.1974

Opposite, left: Biba, printed flanesta dress, Britain, c.1974

Opposite, right: Biba, Art Deco-print brushed cotton dress, Britain, 1974

Opposite, left: Biba, striped wool, cotton and plastic ensemble, Britain, c.1974

Opposite, right: Biba, leopard-print fake-fur coat and cap, Britain, 1973

Left: Biba, man's fun-fur coat, Britain, c.1974

'This was before
people started
looking scruffy
in the evenings.
There was a
moment in
the '70s when
people became
embarrassed
about being
dressed up.'

Left: Biba, striped lamé 'Regency' dress, Britain, c.1974

Opposite, left: Biba, black wool jersey evening dress and jacket, with plastic-sequinned trim, Britain, c.1973

Opposite, right: Biba, crêpe 'Vargas' dress, Britain, c.1973

'At Biba, design evolved. You had this sleeve head, that body, this collar and you'd put them all together like a jigsaw.'

Opposite, left: Biba, black jersey suit with L-shaped Art Deco-style print, Britain, c.1973

Opposite, right: Biba, 1940s-style bonded wool jersey dress, Britain, c.1973

Right: Biba, jersey and fake fur suit, Britain, c.1973

Opposite, left: Biba, purple linen suit, Britain, c.1974

Opposite, right: Biba, polka-dot-print bonded jersey jacket and skirt, Britain, c.1974

Right: Biba, printed wool jersey dress, Britain, 1973

'You had platform shoes, which were hidden under the trousers so the feet were nowhere in sight. It made your legs look 10 feet long, maybe longer!'

Opposite: Biba, grey leopard-print jacquard trouser suit (with fabric detail), Britain, c.1973

Right: Biba, satin-weave cotton trouser suit, Britain, c.1974

Left: Biba, two-piece printed jersey ensemble, Britain, c.1974

Opposite: Biba, chevron-weave wool coat, Britain, c.1974

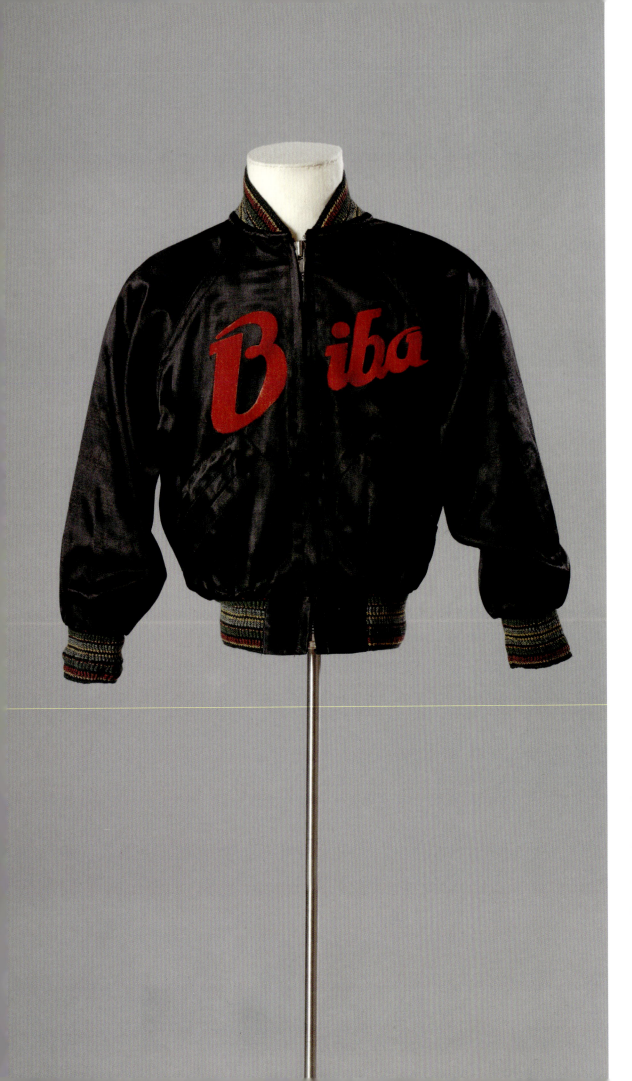

Left: Biba, child's satin-weave cotton bomber jacket, United States, c.1973

Opposite, left: Biba, child's jersey dress, Britain, c.1974

Opposite, right: Biba, child's printed cotton dungarees, Britain, c.1973

'Because the jackets are long, it makes the sleeves look short, but they covered your knuckles and the jackets [covered] your bum. Bums were out!'

Left: Biba, man's wool suit, Britain, c.1974

Opposite, left: Biba, flanesta rayon trouser suit with Art Deco-style print, Britain, c.1974

Opposite, right: Biba, flanesta rayon trouser suit with Art Deco-style print, Britain, c.1974

Beyond Biba

1975–2014

'Barbara, you are an inspiration.'

Kate Moss, 2007[1]

'Biba closes this Autumn and there goes the final nail into the coffin of Swinging London,' reported the *Japan Times* in September 1975.[2] Biba ceased trading on 25 September 1975 and the final act in the Biba story was the sale, managed by Bonhams auction house, of the department store's 'Furnishings, Fixtures, Fittings and Miscellany.'[3] Merchandise became memorabilia, and reports that Biba was to reopen as a smaller concern, returning to its origins as a boutique, were merely the result of wishful thinking from the press, who were unwilling for the story to end.[4]

Although Biba was gone, its influence was inescapable, as the *Observer* acknowledged in 1974: 'Biba ... has been responsible for initiating and subsequently guaranteeing one of the most radical high street revolutions in decades.'[5] The British high street as it emerged in the mid-1970s had absorbed the lessons of Biba, and well-designed clothes for the teenage market were available nationwide. Boutiques that had first appeared in the 1960s within department stores, such as Topshop (1964) and Miss Selfridge (1966), became stand-alone shops in the

1970s, with branches across the country. Affordable fashion littered the high street, with Topshop offering a thigh-length pleated skirt for £4.99, Fenwick selling a striped cotton shirt for £5.50 and a bag from British Home Stores costing only £2.99.[6]

At the time of the closure, Barbara Hulanicki said: 'Biba had been my life, my dream. And [then] it was gone. It was like losing a child – I'm not exaggerating, to me it was as bad as that.'[7] Nor was it just the loss of the shop itself that was painful. 'I went through agony,' she said in 2013. 'Fitz hung on in there, fighting to get the name back, and he kept going to meetings with the money – I think about £5 million – to buy the name. They were having the final meeting and Fitz said, "You're not coming, because they're going to crucify you." I didn't go and he came back and said "Sorry, we've lost."'

In the period immediately following the end of Biba, however, Hulanicki established herself as an independent designer in her own right, under her own name. Lilly Anderson, a friend and Biba girl since the Kensington High Street store, continued working with Hulanicki and Stephen Fitz-Simon and recalls their plan to open a shop called Black Market: 'I always remember Fitz saying to me, "What does black market mean to you?" I said "It's something you can't officially get but you can buy it." It was like getting Barbara's designs on the black market, because they didn't own the Biba name. There was going to be a shop in Westbourne Grove but it never happened ... and then they went to Brazil.'[8]

Realizing that their contract with British Land wouldn't allow them to open a business within 50 miles of London, Hulanicki and Fitz-Simon sought advice from the Chamber

Left: Telegram to Delisia Howard, 19 March 1976

Opposite: Poster for 'Barbara Hulanicki' label, c.1976

of Commerce. Brazil was recommended as a possibility for relocation because of its strong export trade and attractive tax incentives, and the couple moved there with their son Witold in 1976. 'We had just had enough,' Hulanicki said in 1980. 'Brazil seemed different. We didn't know anyone there. We didn't speak the language. We looked out of the window of the Hilton Hotel in São Paulo with people rushing around and thought, gosh, what have we done?'[9]

Initially based in Rio de Janeiro, Hulanicki and Fitz-Simon found the Brazilian working schedule something of a culture shock, as potential business partners would arrive days late and without excuses. They soon moved to São Paulo, Brazil's largest city, where they started the Barbara Hulanicki company with backing from a bank, a deal that Fitz-Simon had negotiated. The Hulanicki label would last from 1976 to 1986, almost as long as Biba itself, trading in womenswear, accessories and childrenswear. T-shirts were a significant part of the business for the domestic market – 'it was always summer there' – and for export, with approximately two million T-shirts sold to the French ready-to-wear label Cacharel and the Italian brand Fiorucci. Both were natural bedfellows for Hulanicki, as they too were creating and selling fashion aimed at the youth market. Hulanicki had admired Cacharel – established in 1964, the same year as the first Biba shop – ever since Rosie Marks, her PA, had worn a green wool Cacharel skirt to work in the mid-1960s. Impressed with the design of the skirt and the quality of the fabric, Hulanicki had considered adapting the pattern for the Biba range. Fiorucci, which opened in Milan in 1967, was very much an Italian Biba, bringing youthful fashion to the country's teenagers. Hulanicki already had a relationship with the label's founder, Elio Fiorucci, as knitwear manufactured by his company had been sold in Big Biba.

Not content with just producing clothes, the couple also opened a shop in Brazil. 'It all started again,' Hulanicki recalls. 'The shop was about 500 square feet. I found this amazing wholesale Lebanese quarter where you could buy accessories and jewellery. I'd buy all this fabulous stuff, all these wonderful belts and bags, and I just filled the shop.' Private houses were again turned into commercial premises, with one building operating as a shop (with

Poster for 'Barbara Hulanicki' label, c.1976. Photo: Ella Dürst.

Return of a fashion legend

A FASHION legend of the Sixties returns to London today with a new operation that will shake-up the fiercely competitive high street fashion world.

Barbara Hulanicki was the designer behind Biba, the store that set the high Art Deco style that dominated the Seventies. While other designers pushed the dolly-bird image, Barbara's customers emerged as pale-lipped vamps pouting behind black veils, wih boas fluttering around satin gowns.

The Biba bubble burst in 1976 with the collapse of an amitious venture at Derry and Toms in Kensington High Street. Barbara and husband, Stephen Fitzsimon, packed up and headed for South America.

After four years in Sao Paolo, Barbara returned to plan the new store in Holland Park Avenue named simply after herself.

She plans to maintain her reputation for high style and low prices.

The new, meticulously planned shop will have no opening celebration. "The doors open at 9.30 am and we're in business," said "Fitz"

BARBARA HULANICKI

Above: 'Return of a fashion legend', *New Standard*, 10 November 1980
Opposite: Magazine advertisement announcing the opening of the Barbara Hulanicki shop in London, *Time Out* (7–13 November 1980)

offices above), another used as a base for production and yet another serving as the family home: 'We would do small runs, sometimes dying the fabric in the washing machines.' The company's products were sold throughout Brazil. 'We had a rep, this Argentinian guy, who would sell millions from the back of his Volkswagen,' Hulanicki says. 'I would spend hours having all the collection beautifully done and he'd just throw it in the back of his boot.'

Boutiques also came to them to buy goods wholesale – an incredibly lucrative prospect for the label, connecting the wealth of fashion consumers in Brazil with European design that was otherwise not imported into the country.

The Hulanicki name, and Barbara's reputation as a leading designer in London in the 1960s and '70s, did not go unnoticed in Brazil, and she was soon designing for an ever-increasing number of people and projects. She designed stage costumes for Marco Nanini, one of Brazil's most famous actors, and for Rita Lee, possibly the nation's most successful singer, with worldwide sales of over 60 million albums. These clothing designs were a continuation of styles she had created for Biba, with long evening wear in satin, sequinned jackets with wide shoulders and Forties-inspired jersey outfits suitable for the South American climate. The fashion shows the Hulanicki label staged attracted a huge amount of press coverage.

During a brief visit to England in the late 1970s, Hulanicki and Fitz-Simon realized that the time was right for the family to return. With Witold boarding at Downside School in Bath, the couple initiated plans to transfer the Hulanicki label from South America to Europe.

The Hulanicki label eventually reached London in 1980, in the form of a stand-alone shop. Hulanicki and Fitz-Simon's old friend, the clothing manufacturer Wally Rose, provided the perfect opportunity. 'He owned a group of shops and he kept giving us these men's shops that didn't work for him,' Hulanicki recalls. Occupying a former bank on Holland Park Avenue, the relatively modest shop opened on 10 November 1980. Fitz-Simon explained the small-scale launch in an interview at the time: 'Last time we began small [on Abingdon Road] because we had no money. This time we have financial backing, but we have learnt that keeping fixed costs down is the key to survival. We have found that the average newcomer spends about 50 per cent more on a shop front than we [have] on the whole shop.'[10]

The launch of the shop was met with a flurry of media interest: 'Return of a fashion legend' announced the *New Standard* (above),[11] 'Barbara (ex-Biba) bounces back' explained *The Sunday Times*[12] and the *Daily Telegraph* celebrated 'A new shop, a new name, a new look…'[13] Fashion stories appeared in *Ritz* magazine and *Time Out*, while *Cosmopolitan* devoted eight pages to the new venture. 'Barbara Hulanicki is back in town banking on fashion you can afford,' the magazine declared. '[The shop] is full of wonderfully easy clothes, whose special charms are their texture – suede, glossy leather, canvas, jersey – and their colour – cream, khaki, indigo, violet … this is the best

Opening on Monday, November 10th

BARBARA
HULANICKI

124, Holland Park Avenue, W.11.

thing to happen to fashion for years.'[14] The article listed jersey tops that sold for £5.95, with matching trousers at £9.55, as well as leather jackets at £34.99, suede boots for £15 and a leather shoulder bag at £8.65.

Customers expecting a new Biba, however, were in for a disappointment. Hulanicki's designs reflected the market for women in their twenties and older, who wanted smart, wearable outfits, rather than quirky clothes for teenagers. London was once again booming in 1980, with small boutiques already offering unique clothes for the teenagers who would have been Biba customers in the 1960s and '70s. In November 1980 PX in Endell Street sold 'romantic, flamboyant and utterly extravagant' clothing for both sexes, while Swanky Modes on Camden Road was offering 'lurid pink tweed suits'.[15] Seditionaries, Vivienne Westwood and Malcolm McLaren's shop on King's Road and the spiritual

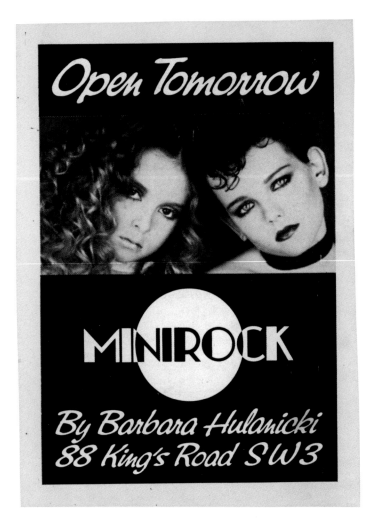

home of street fashion, closed in 1980 before reopening in its latest and last incarnation as World's End. What hadn't changed from the Biba days was Hulanicki's philosophy regarding inexpensive fashion. 'I find it difficult to believe anyone can spend £500 on a dress; to me that's the price of a car,' she said in 1985.[16] The suede boots featured in the *Cosmopolitan* article were nearly half the price of a similar design by the Katrina label, which sold for £49.95, and £10 cheaper than a pair of suede moccasin boots by Midas.[17]

The trouser suit had evolved in design throughout Biba's history, from the slightly masculine style of the 1964 pinstripe suit (pp.38–9) to form-fitting styles in printed cotton in 1974 (p.209). The late 1970s had once again seen the rise of the shoulder pad, with designers such as Claude Montana and Thierry Mugler creating square-shouldered suit jackets, heralding what was to become a key look for the 1980s. Androgyny was also in vogue with pop stars of the day, most famously Culture Club's Boy George and the crop-haired Annie Lennox, singer with the Eurythmics. Grace Jones appeared on the cover of her 1981 album, *Nightclubbing*, wearing only a square-shouldered black Armani jacket, sporting a flat-top haircut and with a cigarette hanging from her lips – a new form of femininity for a new decade. Hulanicki's check wool trouser suit (c.1983) is the most masculine womenswear design of her career, with turn-ups on the trousers and no bust darts on the square-shouldered jacket (p.232). The only discernible feminine feature is the right-over-left buttoning.

The first, and successful, Hulanicki shop was quickly followed by another, which opened at 245 Regent Street in 1981. A third shop, devoted entirely to childrenswear, was launched in September 1981 at 88 King's Road (left): building on the principles first laid down at Biba on Kensington Church Street, the concept of young shoppers making personal clothing choices was taken to its natural conclusion in this store. In Brazil, Hulanicki had created a children's range called the Stork Club, which in London evolved into the label, and then the shop, MINIROCK. Under this label, she designed collections exclusively for the Japanese market (a market Hulanicki and Fitz-Simon understood well from their experience with Biba cosmetics, and where they had trusted business contacts).

Advertising flyer for MINIROCK childrenswear shop, c.1981

Barbara Hulanicki, sketches for cosmetics colours and looks, work on paper, 1983

Hulanicki also continued to work as a design consultant for Elio Fiorucci's company during this period: 'I went to their offices in Milan once a month – just designing clothes, collections. It was really interesting; there must have been about 20 designers from every part of the world: Japan was very big then, French designers, Italian designers, American designers … amazing offices and facilities. Fiorucci loved designers.' The 1980s were Fiorucci's most commercially successful decade and Hulanicki's collections for the brand were in keeping with

her aesthetic for her own label, relevant to 'today' rather than a backward glance at her previous design work.

Biba products were still available on Britain's high streets in the early 1980s, with Dorothy Perkins selling the cosmetics nationwide in their shops. The continuing success of Biba cosmetics was a factor in the decision to produce a Hulanicki cosmetics range. A workbook in the

Above: Barbara Hulanicki cosmetics from 1983

Opposite: Promotional image for Hulanicki cosmetics, c.1983.
Photo: James Wedge.

company's archive in Miami, dated November 1982, details the range of colours, each one given its own identifying name (as on previous page). Eye shadow colours include 'Fireball', 'Beam', 'Radium' and 'Goblin' (scarlet, turquoise, fuchsia and jade respectively). Gold, silver and bronze are represented (named 'Alchemy', 'Chalice' and 'Syn'), as are the colours typically associated with Barbara Hulanicki – 'Merlin' (bilberry), 'Wode [sic]' (blue), 'Hades' (brown) and 'Witch' (purple). Of the 18 lipsticks, three were in classic Hulanicki colours – purple, green and a reddish-brown. The majority of the lipsticks,

however, were from her 1980s colour palette, with bright reds ('Banshee') and pinks ('Fetish'), anticipating the market for traditional cosmetic colours (left), with another contemporary example being Miss Selfridge's popular lipstick, the pillar-box red 'Doris Karloff'.

Launched in the autumn of 1983, the cosmetics were inexpensive, with lipsticks selling for £2.65, blushers for £5.85 and nail varnish for £1.99. *Elle* magazine later described the range as a 'breakthrough line of vibrant cosmetics, sheathed in silver and ready to take off for the beauty stratosphere … this electric, eclectic collection contains provocative colours like Strobe (blusher), Oboy (mini-blusher), Flo (lipstick and gloss) and Shock (nail polish).'[18] Hulanicki remembers, 'We had a really big warehouse and we ran the cosmetics, which were all made in England. We did everything ourselves. We were in Topshop, the Body Shop, [New York department store] Macy's, Judy's [in Los Angeles], H&M – that was really big business in Sweden and Germany.' Hulanicki cosmetics were also sold in independent shops across the country, with the silver and black containers displayed on striking Art Deco-style mirrored display stands – a nod to her style in the Biba years.

By the mid-1980s, the stand-alone Barbara Hulanicki shops had closed as the cosmetics business grew, but the designer was branching out in other ways. 'The thing with cosmetics is [that] you do it twice a year: you go to your factory and you mix your colours. That wasn't enough for me, so I had to do other things,' Hulanicki explains. 'Fitz said, "You should get back into drawing, because it's going to be needed." He could see that computers were taking over design.'

Hulanicki's illustrations had always reflected the fashionable looks and body types of the period: her early work showing the influence of her idol Audrey Hepburn, with Cathy McGowan taking over as her muse in the mid-1960s and Ingrid Boulting the model 'Biba girl' in the 1970s. In the 1980s, her illustrations reflected the more exotic looks of contemporary models such as Talisa Soto and Yasmin Le Bon (p.223). Hulanicki took on high-profile commissions, including producing an illustration of the dress Sarah Ferguson wore on her wedding to Prince Andrew, on 23 July 1986, for the cover of the *Evening Standard*. She also took up photography

HIDDEN ASSETS

OF course, it's one thing pouring yourself into these wonderful, slinky little numbers but it's quite another knowing what to wear underneath to enhance your shape as well as disguise ugly knicker lines.

The perfect outfit requires the perfect underwear

High-waisted knickers are an essential accessory to wear under tight trousers. Available from Gossard, £4.99. Support tights (worn without briefs) also avoid the knicker line. Elbeo, from £2.50

Body-shapers are excellent for accentuating the waistline and give that much sought-after Joan Collins look. Gossard, £19.99

Revitalise your old sweaters with vests complete with shoulder pads. Fenwick, £6.95

Hold that bulge with an all-in-one bodysuit from Charnos, £24.95. The stitching under the bust line emphasises the new curvaceous shape

Opposite: Editorial fashion feature, c.1986. Photo: Barbara Hulanicki.

Above: 'Hidden Assets', with fashion illustrations by Barbara Hulanicki, *She* magazine (February 1987)

again, more for creative fulfillment than as a profession, although she received numerous commissions for portraits, photographing the likes of actor Anthony Hopkins and her friends Twiggy and Ronnie Wood, and for newspaper fashion editorials (opposite).

Hulanicki's skill and experience in creating interiors for the Biba shops made her move into interior design, though unplanned, almost inevitable. While she was producing collections for Cacharel in Paris, the company's founder Jean Bousquet invited her to design a showroom. '[It was]

this amazing building, an old warehouse that he had his Paris offices in,' Hulanicki explains. 'He said, "Could you just put it together and make it into a showroom?" So I did the interior design, going round Paris getting everything really cheap. He said to me, "Would you like to stay and do the whole building?" and I thought, No. It had never occurred to me I should be doing something like that.'

A combination of intuition and fortuitous circumstance were to lead to a two-decade career in interior design. In the mid-1980s, Ronnie Wood, the guitarist for the Rolling Stones, asked Hulanicki to design the interior of his club in South Beach, near Miami. Hulanicki remembers, 'I never did a drawing. I just did it with chalk on the floor, marking out, say, where the stage had

to be, and then some musician would come down and say, "No, the stage has got the go there", so we'd rip out everything and start again.' The club, Woody's on the Beach, was originally scheduled to take six months to complete but Hulanicki was to find that, as in Brazil, 'in Miami things go slow.' Woody's eventually took over two years to finish, by which time Hulanicki and Fitz-Simon had fallen in love with South Beach and Miami: 'Little did we realize it was all very dodgy, with Miami built on drug money.'

In 1990, Hulanicki met Chris Blackwell, the owner of Island Records. Blackwell recalls: 'Barbara and I met when Island Records were doing a video in Miami and, to my shock and surprise, there was the iconic Barbara Hulanicki doing the styling! The art director Tony Wright ... had found out she was in Miami and had contacted her. I asked Barbara if she would work on the interior design for the Marlin Hotel on South Beach (opposite). She did the most unbelievable job – the opening of the Marlin garnered such a massive amount of international press that to this day it is considered the spark that started the revival of South Beach.'[19] Blackwell went on to purchase 11 derelict buildings in the South Beach neighbourhood, which were transformed by Hulanicki into some of the first boutique hotels, each with a quirky, individual identity. In 1993, she designed the interiors of the Cavalier Hotel, the Kent Hotel and the Leslie Hotel, and her work on the interiors of the Netherland, an Art Deco apartment building (right), won her an award from the American Institute of Architects in 1993. The informal way of working in Miami was a practice with which Hulanicki was unfamiliar: 'suddenly the landscape gardener started to get involved with the interiors and I can't put up with that, so I resigned.' Hulanicki's resigning from jobs had become part of the process while working with Blackwell, earning her the nickname 'Design and Resign'. She always returned to finish the job – her resignations were more of a protest – but it was during a more definite episode of 'Design and Resign' that Hulanicki and Fitz-Simon started their final business venture together.

Witold Fitz-Simon was by now living in New York, having studied film at New York University's Tisch School of the Arts, and his parents were keen to join him. 'We were just following him around,' Hulanicki admits. The couple planned to open a shop in downtown

Opposite: Marlin Hotel, South Beach, Florida, c.1990

Above: Hulanicki at the Netherland building, South Beach, Florida, c.1993

Manhattan selling womenswear and accessories and, fittingly, the name of the new business was to reflect almost four decades of partnership: Fitz & Fitz.

'We were setting up the shop in New York, everything was gorgeous, and then we discovered Fitz had cancer,' Hulanicki remembers. 'We were living at the Chelsea Hotel at the time and everything was coming on – the shop, production. He had a terrible pain down his side, like sciatica, and he began going to a therapist. This went on for about three weeks but it wasn't getting better, so he went to see a neurologist, who put him into hospital immediately. Witold and I went to collect him but they wanted to keep him in for observation and some intern comes up to me and says casually, "Your husband's got three months to live." And then we had to go and face Fitz.'

Leaving New York, the whole family returned to Miami for Fitz-Simon's radiotherapy and chemotherapy treatments. These were unsuccessful and he died on 16 January 1997, aged 59: 'Such a terrible, terrible time.

It was a shock. He wasn't supposed to die.' In the obituary, which was published in London a few days later, Liz Smith wrote: 'Fitz relished the cut and thrust of running his retail empire. The day-to-day disasters that dog any venture were treated as a potential source of good-natured amusement. A warm, friendly man – and generous to a fault – he could be prickly and sharp in business deals, able to slug out any deal to his own satisfaction. He appreciated toughness in others too. When Barbara complained about a particularly overbearing employee Fitz had employed, he said, "I know he's a right bastard, but that's what we need."'[20] Ten years earlier, Fitz-Simon had said: '[Business] is literally a battle to the death, and the last man standing wins the game. So whatever happens, keep going and you will get there. Once you stop you are lost. It is that simple and that hard. Personally I'm a great believer in prayer.'[21]

Chris Blackwell asked Hulanicki to return to work with him in 1997 and, surrounded by friends and familiar faces, she picked up where she had left off. It was through Blackwell that Hulanicki met Likrish Marchese, who became, initially, her personal assistant and then her trusted second-in-command. Marchese recalls her first few weeks of working with Hulanicki in Miami: 'I literally couldn't keep up with her. She'd be off and I'd have to try and keep up. And I was in my twenties. Barbara worked all the time, and eventually I had to say, "Can I please have at least one weekend off?"'

With a career in fashion and design spanning half a century, Hulanicki was able to bring her wealth of experience, store of design knowledge and intuitive understanding of fashion trends to a whole host of companies in the twenty-first century. She would be more productive and travel more extensively than ever before, associating the Hulanicki name with interiors, homeware and home furnishings as well as the whole range of fashion products – clothes, shoes, bags. Since launching the Hulanicki label in Brazil in 1976, she has collaborated with established companies, designing products or ranges that she deems appropriate for her company. As a natural extension of her interior design work, Hulanicki began designing a range of wallpapers and paints for the British company Graham & Brown in 2007 (below, right). The paint range includes

Opposite: Hulanicki and Fitz-Simon in the Fitz & Fitz boutique in New York, c.1996

Below, left: Barbara Hulanicki, 'banana' wallpaper designed for the 1996 Habitat *VIP* collection

Below, right: Barbara Hulanicki, wallpaper designed for Graham & Brown, c.2009

some classic Hulanicki colours – wine-coloured purples and rusty browns – and flock wallpapers are decorated with her prints in Pugin, Art Nouveau and Art Deco-inspired designs. Coccinelle, the luxury Italian leather goods company, asked Hulanicki to design bags for a number of seasons, starting in 2008.

Hulanicki's return to fashion design came through a chance meeting at the private view of her 2008 exhibition of fine-art illustrations, held at the Coningsby Gallery in London. The event was attended by a designer at Topshop, who invited her to design a collection for the store. Asked to create around 50 possible designs for the collection, Hulanicki's prodigious productivity eventually saw her produce 125, which were whittled down to the required number. Her designs were contemporary to 2010, with little or no reference to her work for Biba or even the Hulanicki label. A grey suede jacket, one of Hulanicki's favourites from the collection, has Biba-esque shoulders but is also in keeping with the revival of exaggerated shoulders sparked by Balmain's military-style 'hussar' jacket of 2008. The capsule collection of 30 garments also included 1940s-inspired beachwear, a 1950s-style cotton prom dress (p.236) and printed chiffon blouses. Launched on 28 April 2009, the collection was described by *Vogue* as 'flirty and floaty ... in coral, pink and turquoise tones', and garments from the range were worn by young fashion icons including Alexa Chung, Mary-Kate Olsen and Peaches Geldof, among others.[22]

In the 1960s, Hulanicki had looked back to the 1930s for design inspiration, a period some 30 years in the past, and now designers were looking to the equally distant designs of the 1960s and '70s, with Biba an iconic name in the annals of British fashion. Kate Moss based a knitted dress from her 2007 collection for Topshop on a Biba jumper from 1970. The jumper had originally belonged to Lilly Anderson, a Biba girl and friend of Hulanicki's. Anderson gave it to her best friend, hairdresser Sam McKnight, who in turn gave it to Kate Moss. The Biba jumper had laddered at the neck, so when Moss designed her own version, she re-created the jumper complete with the ladders, changing the neckline and the length to create a jumper dress (p.237). Biba originals, by the 2000s, were themselves highly collectable – a jacquard coat with matching trousers and hat, which retailed in 1974 for £25,

£8.95 and £3.50 respectively, sold for just under £2,000 at auction in 2013.

Since Hulanicki and Fitz-Simon's loss of the Biba name itself in 1975, it has been bought and sold several times and attached to numerous re-launches, never with Barbara Hulanicki's involvement or approval. The first re-launch, in 1977, saw Hulanicki's sister Biruta, 'Biba', design for a shop that opened on London's Conduit Street. It lasted just two years before closing. The 1990s saw another revival, with Monica Zipper as head designer and a store in Covent Garden. The clothes, although not adhering to the Biba aesthetic, were reasonably priced. In 2006, the name was bought again, this time by Michael Pearce, who relaunched Biba as a high-end fashion label with Bella Freud as head designer. Original Biba prints, such as the Pugin print from 1964 and the Maltese cross print from 1968, were used on garments and accessories, and Biba signature fabrics such as satin, crêpe and lace were used. Freud left the label after two seasons, in June 2007. The latest incarnation of the name is House of Fraser's Biba boutique, positioned within their department stores nationwide. Launched in September 2010, their current label is trading very successfully at the time of print.

In 2010, Hulanicki began designing a range of women's clothes for supermarket clothing label George at Asda (pp.233, 238–9). This collaboration took her back to the ethic of Biba years: producing a constant stream of designs, all to be sold for under £20 (many for under £10). 'I design in Miami and then go over for fittings every six weeks,' Hulanicki explains. 'At first I was going to London, but they've opened new offices and a production site in Turkey, which are amazing. They've got that Eastern element and are incredibly design-wise, coupled with really good taste.' The clothes reflect Hulanicki's life in design, with wide-shouldered and puff-sleeved dresses in William Morris-esque, Art Nouveau and leopard prints. As much as Hulanicki has staunchly avoided re-creating designs from her past, it is only since perhaps 2010 that she has come to recognize the importance of the style and power of the retail phenomenon she and Fitz-Simon created in Biba. A blue jersey T-shirt dress from her 2012 George collection (p.239, left) is an adaptation of a

Signed photo sent to Hulanicki from Kate Moss, c.2007

Dear Barbara, You are an inspiration. Thankyou. With love, yours Kate ♡

Dress Kate Moss Topshop. Knickers What Katie Did. Shoes Christian Louboutin.

1965 design, only now in stretch jersey rather than cotton – re-designed to make it appropriate for today's market.

Icon Club, launched in summer 2014, is Hulanicki's own label, which sells T-shirts, bags and scarves printed with her illustrations. 'It's all produced in London and it comes back to drawing and illustration,' she explains. 'At the time when Fitz suggested it, I was like, "… I don't want to get back into drawing", but he plants ideas in your head, you know. He was terribly clever. Thanks, Fitz.'

In the 2010 film *Made in Dagenham*, which tells the story of the 1968 strike among female sewing machinists at the Ford Motor Company's plant in Essex, a red linen Biba dress symbolizes the film's themes of female equality and emancipation in 1960s Britain. The Biba dress, which belongs to the middle-class, Cambridge-educated character Lisa Hopkins (played by Rosamund Pike), is admired by working-class Ford machinist Rita O'Grady (played by Sally Hawkins). On winning their fight for equal pay, O'Grady presents herself to the media in the borrowed Biba dress, underlining the rewards of her now-increased economic power as well as acknowledging the commonality of all women.

Hulanicki and Fitz-Simon's Biba had always striven to embody democratic ideals. Their customers included royalty, celebrities and shop girls, and the company's business practices sought to support under-represented sections of society. Biba was the first high-street retailer to offer well-designed clothes at prices accessible to all; it offered the first make-up range for black skin; it made cosmetics for men; it actively supported the nascent gay community by advertising in the gay press; and it understood the lives of modern working women. In Kensington in the 1960s, Brazil in the 1970s, Miami in the 1980s, Hulanicki's philosophy has always been innovation and experimentation, underpinned by intuition – her ability to tune into trends and ideas before they materialize in mainstream culture.

Biba's contribution to fashion history will be the ultra-skinny silhouette: 'Long torso, flat chest, thin arms, low waist and straight hips.' The Biba retail revolution will be its legacy: retail as theatre, consumerism as a leisure activity, the company name attached to lifestyle as well as products. Biba was a product and symptom of post-war consumer society. In an overwhelmingly corporate world, it was an experiment and, more significantly, an experience that will never be repeated.

Biba is dead: long live Biba.

Barbara Hulanicki wearing a Biba jumper, c.1970. Photo: James Wedge.

Left: Barbara Hulanicki, checked wool trouser suit, Britain, c.1983

Opposite, left: Barbara Hulanicki, blue heart-print polyester-mix dress for George at Asda, Turkey, 2012

Opposite, right: Barbara Hulanicki, printed viscose jersey wrapover dress for George at Asda, Turkey, 2012

Left: Barbara Hulanicki, child's cotton dress, Britain, 1982

Opposite, left: Barbara Hulanicki, leopard-print viscose crêpe dress for Topshop, India, 2009

Opposite, right: Barbara Hulanicki, viscose chiffon dress for Topshop, India, 2009

'Topshop
were so good
to work with.
They worked
amazingly well,
like Biba.
They knew
their shapes.'

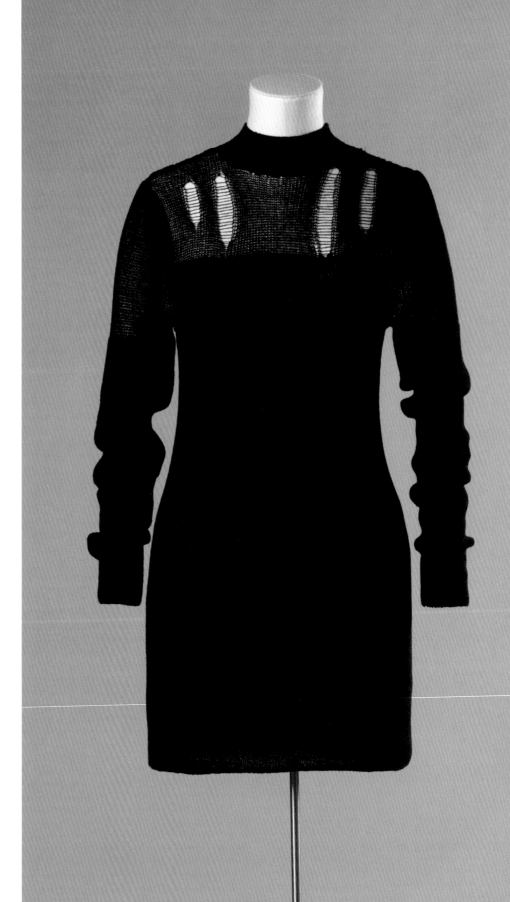

Opposite: Barbara Hulanicki, lilac prom dress for Topshop, India, c.2009

Right: Kate Moss, Biba-inspired jumper dress for Topshop, India, 2010

'That's a real Biba cut. The shoulders are wide, with a long torso and tight sleeves.'

Left: Barbara Hulanicki, leopard-print dress for George at Asda, Turkey, c.2011

Opposite, left: Barbara Hulanicki, T-shirt dress for George at Asda, Turkey, c.2012

Opposite, right: Barbara Hulanicki, blue dress with white and red details for George at Asda, Turkey, c.2012

The Biba Look

Illustrations by Barbara Hulanicki

1963 Simple shapes – mid-length shift dresses and smocks – predominate, in basic, block-colour or printed cottons. High armholes, a flat bust and long torso characterize the silhouette.

1964 Development of shift dresses and smocks with shaped sleeves (funnel, balloon), and maxi dresses in Art Nouveau or Gothic Revival-inspired prints.

1965 Thigh-length jackets and coats with square shoulders are produced in printed cottons, as well as heavier materials such as corduroy and fur.

1966 Long Regency-style gowns, with high necks and bishop sleeves, demonstrate the influence of historical fashion on Biba designs, and are produced in printed and plain cottons. This year also sees the introduction of large, puffed sleeve heads, creating a wide-shouldered silhouette.

1968 Tailored fit is emphasized on short jackets and skirts, and fitted suits and coats. Wide shoulders, pleated sleeve heads and long, tight sleeves give the arm a distinctive shape.

Mini-dresses also appear in wool (with T-strap), and jersey and cotton (round-necked). Sleeves are tight-fitting, with pleated sleeve heads.

Fitted shapes emerge: suits with trousers, skirts or culottes, in wool and cotton lace. Hulanicki also designs jumpsuits with knee- or ankle-length trousers in printed cottons.

1970 The '1930s vamp' look: floor-length, figure-hugging dresses with large, billowing sleeves and plunging necklines made in satins and crêpes.

1971–2 Wide trousers completely covering platform shoes create the illusion of height and a long-line silhouette. Garments are characterized by a square shoulder line and tight sleeves.

1973–4 Padded and rounded shoulders, long jackets (reaching to the thighs) and knuckle-length sleeves create a relaxed, 1940s-style shape. Coats are long or three-quarter length with wide sleeves.

Notes

†   Unless otherwise stated, all pull quotes are from a series of interviews with Barbara Hulanicki, held on 3 and 27 June 2013; 1, 2, 3 and 28 July 2013; and 9 and 19 October 2013.

A number of quotes in this book are taken from press clippings in the Biba archive, Miami. The publisher has made every effort to include complete references but, where this has not been possible, the reader is directed to the relevant date of publication.

INTRODUCTION

1.   Interview with Louise Prince, 19 November 2012

BECOMING BIBA
1936–1963

1.   Thomas Hardy, 'The Ghost of the Past', in James Gibson (ed.), *Thomas Hardy: The Complete Poems* (Basingstoke 2001), p.308
2.   Barbara Hulanicki, *A to Biba* (London 2007), p.12
3.   Unless otherwise stated, all Barbara Hulanicki quotes, here and throughout, are from a series of interviews with the author, held on 3 and 27 June 2013; 1, 2, 3 and 28 July 2013; and 9 and 19 October 2013.
4.   'My Kind of Book', *Petticoat* (30 July 1966), p.9
5.   Interview with Alicia Bregman, née Bradford, 9 August 2013
6.   Mary Quant, *Quant by Quant* (London 2012), p.38
7.   Virginia Ironside, *Janey and Me: Growing Up with My Mother* (London 2003), p.128
8.   Ibid., p.130
9.   Interview with Jennie Peel, née Dingemans, 24 May 2012
10.   Interview with Jo D'Arcy, née Dingemans, 24 May 2012
11.   Interview with Jennie Peel (cited note 9)
12.   Interview with Pauline Ratty, 7 April 2012
13.   Hulanicki (cited note 2), p.50

87 ABINGDON ROAD
1964–1966

1.   Twiggy Lawson and Penelope Denning, *Twiggy In Black and White* (London 1997), pp.32–3
2.   Dominic Sandbrook, *White Heat: A History of Britain in the Swinging Sixties* (London 2006), p.4
3.   Cited in Ruth Lynam (ed.), *Paris Fashion, The Great Designers and their Creations* (London 1972), p.200
4.   Ibid.
5.   Interview with Felicity Green, 26 August 2012
6.   *Daily Mirror*, 1 May 1964, p.17
7.   Ibid.
8.   *Sunday Telegraph*, 21 June 1964, p.14
9.   Ibid.
10.   Interview with Barbara Hulanicki, *c*.1972, Barbara Hulanicki archive, Miami
11.   Interview with Barbara Griggs, 1 April 2013
12.   Ibid.
13.   Figure taken from Barbara Hulanicki, *A to Biba* (London 2007), p.72
14.   Interview with Julie Hodgess, 21 October 2012
15.   Cited in Marwick (cited note 10), p.46
16.   Sandbrook (cited note 2), p.102
17.   Interview with Victor Edelstein, 9 February 2013
18.   Arthur Marwick, *The Sixties* (Oxford 1998), p.60
19.   It has been suggested (by George Melly and Iain R. Webb respectively) that Mary Quant and Foale & Tuffin exemplified the Pop art ethos, but both fall down as regards low cost and Foale & Tuffin did not engage in mass production. Quant started her Ginger Group in America in 1963, for mass production of her designs.
20.   'National Prize', *She* (October 1964), p.63
21.   Interview with Barbara Griggs (cited note 11)
22.   *Daily Mail*, 24 March 1966
23.   *Woman's Mirror*, 2 April 1966, p.31
24.   Interview with Sarah Plunkett, 10 April 2013
25.   Interview with Rosie Bartlett, née Marks, 6 October 2013

26.   Interview with Julie Hodgess (cited note 14)
27.   Virginia Ironside, *Janey and Me: Growing Up with My Mother* (London 2003), p.133
28.   Mary Quant, *Quant by Quant* (London 2012), p.39
29.   Interview with Annie Hawker, 30 July 2013
30.   Ibid.
31.   *Sun*, 27 June 1967
32.   Cited in Paolo Hewitt, *The Sharper Word: A Mod Anthology* (London 2007), p.97
33.   Interview with James Wedge, 20 May 2013
34.   *Daily Mail*, 8 October 2009, p.58
35.   Interview with Sarah Plunkett (cited note 24)
36.   'Clan Clothes For You', *Rave* (November 1964), pp.34–5, 38
37.   'Dressing on the Breadline', *Nova* (July 1965), vol.1, no.5, pp.60–8
38.   Anjelica Huston, *A Story Lately Told: Coming of Age in Ireland* (London and New York), p.144
39.   'After the Frost', *Petticoat* (4 March 1967), no.55, pp.18–19
40.   *Evening Argus*, 4 November 1965
41.   Interview with Hilary Masters, 17 May 2012

19–21 KENSINGTON CHURCH STREET
1966–1969

1.   Correspondence with Annie Lennox, 19 July 2013
2.   *Daily Mail*, 28 February 1966
3.   Dominic Sandbrook, *White Heat: A History of Britain in the Swinging Sixties* (London 2006), p.650
4.   Barbara Hulanicki, *A to Biba* (London 2007), p.85
5.   *Evening News*, 28 February 1966, p.4
6.   Interview with Julie Hodgess, 21 October 2012
7.   John Russell, 'Reviews and Previews', *Art News* (October 1966), vol.65, no.6, p.19
8.   Interview with Antony Little, 10 September 2011
9.   'My Kind of Book', *Petticoat* (30 July 1966), p.9
10.   *The Times*, 30 October 1967, p.7
11.   'London: The Swinging City', *Time* (15 April 1966), pp.34–5
12.   Ibid.
13.   *Daily Mirror*, 17 May 1967, p.14
14.   'Letter from London', *Petticoat* (9 September 1967), no.82, p.37
15.   Paolo Hewitt, *The Sharper Word: A Mod Anthology* (London 2007), p.97
16.   Interview with Barbara Griggs, 1 April 2013
17.   Valerie Steele, *Paris Fashion: A Cultural History* (Oxford 1999), p.279
18.   Letter to Felicity Green from Penny Portair, dated 13 April 1967, Barbara Hulanicki archive, Miami
19.   Letter from M. De Guillage, director of the Office de coordination économique, to Stephen Fitz-Simon, 18 January 1967, Barbara Hulanicki archive, Miami
20.   'It's Gear on the Rocks … as Biba, Birds and Beat Move Into Zermatt', *London Look* (14 January 1967), pp.9–11
21.   Interview with Victor Edelstein, 9 February 2013
22.   Interview with Sarah Plunkett, 10 April 2013
23.   *Daily Mail*, 14 August 1967
24.   'Once Upon a Willow Tree', *Vogue* (July 1968), vol.124, no.7, p.73
25.   Interview with Jo D'Arcy, née Dingemans, 24 May 2012
26.   *The Star*, Jamaica, 14 October 1967
27.   Interview with Jo D'Arcy, née Dingemans (cited note 25)
28.   Since 2008, the logo has appeared on accessories by Roberto Cavalli and, in a redesigned form, on a John Galliano T-shirt.
29.   Interview with Maddie Smith, 15 March 2012
30.   Stephen Fitz-Simon, *Being the Boss* (London 1987), p.50
31.   Interview with John McConnell, 18 February 2012
32.   Hepburn's costumes were eventually designed by a number of different designers, including Mary Quant and André Courrèges.
33.   Interview with Delisia Howard, 13 May 2012
34.   Ibid.
35.   Interview with Julie Hodgess (cited note 6)
36.   *Observer Magazine* (19 January 1969), pp.18–19
37.   Ibid.
38.   Ibid.

120 KENSINGTON HIGH STREET
1969–1973

1. 'The Bird's Nest', *Women's Wear Daily*, 4 December 1969, pp.4–5
2. *The Observer*, 14 September 1969
3. Interview with Lilly Anderson, 2 June 2013
4. Biba's 'purple press pack', London, 1969, p.2
5. Interview with Lilly Anderson (cited note 3)
6. Interview with Sarah Plunkett, 10 August 2013
7. Interview with Julie Hodgess, 21 October 2012
8. 'The Bird's Nest' (cited note 1), p.4
9. Interview with Lilly Anderson, 2 October 2013
10. Barney Hoskyns, *Glam!: Bowie, Bolan and the Glitter Revolution* (London 1998), p.6
11. Interview with Lilly Anderson (cited note 9)
12. 'The Bird's Nest' (cited note 1), pp.4–5
13. Biba's 'purple press pack' (cited note 4), p.5
14. Interview with Victor Edelstein, 9 February 2013
15. Interview with Jo D'Arcy, née Dingemans, 24 May 2012
16. 'The Rise and Rise of the Biba Girl', *Petticoat* (October 1973)
17. Interview with Delisia Howard, 13 May 2012
18. Letter to Barbara Hulanicki, dated 24 September 1971, Biba archive, Miami
19. Letter to Cardinelli Beauty Products Ltd from Delisia Howard, dated 2 November 1971, Biba archive, Miami
20. Letter to Cardinelli Beauty Products Ltd from Delisia Howard, dated 13 July 1972, Biba archive, Miami
21. Interview with Barbara Hulanicki, *c*.1972, Barbara Hulanicki archive, Miami
22. 'Breathes there the man with soul so dead / Who never to himself hath said, / "This is my own, my native land!"' Sir Walter Scott, 'The Lay of the Last Minstrel', 1805
23. *Daily Record*, 17 November 1967
24. *Daily Express*, 14 August 1967, p.4
25. Interview with Jo D'Arcy, née Dingemans (cited note 15)
26. *Drapery and Fashion Weekly* (29 January 1971)
27. Interview with Jennie Peel, 24 May 2013
28. All quotes from Biba promotional pack, *Seventeen* magazine for McCalls patterns, USA, 1970
29. Interview with Jo D'Arcy, née Dingemans (cited note 15)
30. *The Sunday Times*, 17 January 1971
31. *Observer*, 21 December 1969, p.3
32. Barbara Hulanicki, *A to Biba* (London 2007), p.121
33. *Fashion: An Anthology by Cecil Beaton*, exh. cat., Victoria and Albert Museum, London (London 1971), p.54
34. Cited in Tom Vague, *Anarchy in the UK* (Oakland, CA 1997), p.51
35. 'Twiggy in Bibaland', *Vogue* (December 1973), vol.130, no.16, p.138

BIG BIBA, 99–117 KENSINGTON HIGH STREET
1973–1975

1. Cited in Barney Hoskyns, *Glam!: Bowie, Bolan and the Glitter Revolution* (London 1998), p.86
2. *Guardian*, 11 April 1974
3. Interview with Steven Thomas, 27 May 2013
4. *The New Yorker*, cited in Steven Thomas and Alwyn W. Turner, *Welcome to Big Biba: Inside the Most Beautiful Store in the World* (Woodbridge 2006), p.72
5. *The Sunday Mirror*, 6 September 1973
6. *Glass Age* (November 1973)
7. *Procurement* (February 1974)
8. *Estate Times*, 22 November 1973
9. *Japan Times*, 4 November 1973
10. 'Twiggy in Bibaland', *Vogue* (December 1973), vol.130, no.16, pp.138–43
11. Ibid.
12. 'We're Just Good Furriends', *Nova* (January 1974), p.34
13. *Daily Express*, 19 November 1974
14. Cited in Alfred K. Ho, *Achieving the American Dream* (London 2007), p.12
15. Dominic Sandbrook, *State of Emergency: The Way We Were, Britain 1970–1974* (London 2011), p.3
16. Biba newspaper, 10 September 1973, p.4, Biba archive, Miami

17. *Circus* (April 1975)
18. Interview with Allan Gearing, 10 September 2013
19. Biba newspaper (cited note 16), p.6
20. *Mother & Baby* (February 1974), p.12
21. *Daily Express*, 24 January 1974
22. Ann Price, 'A Certain Style', *Country Life* (27 December 1973), vol.154, no.3992, pp.2194–5
23. 'What fits Fitz, fits Biba', *Evening Standard*, 10 July 1974, p.24
24. Steven Thomas and Alwyn W. Turner, *Welcome to Big Biba* (London 2006), p.33
25. *Daily Express*, 27 May 1974, p.11
26. Cited in Hoskyns (cited note 1), p.86
27. 'Hello Hollywood!', *Evening News*, 26 September 1974, p.6
28. Ibid.
29. Ibid.
30. Ibid.
31. Interview with Lilly Anderson, 2 October 2013
32. *The Director* (March 1974)
33. 'What Fits Fitz, fits Biba' (cited note 23), p.24
34. Ibid.
35. Interview with Lorraine Harper, 15 April 2013
36. Steven Fitz-Simon, *Being the Boss* (London 1987), p.27. Fitz also mentions stealing at another department store's boutique department, which was running at 18 per cent.
37. Interview with James Wedge, 20 May 2013
38. 'The day Mrs Biba left a dream world behind', *Evening News*, 12 September 1975

BEYOND BIBA
1975–2014

1. Letter from Kate Moss to Barbara Hulanicki, June 2007
2. *Japan Times*, September 1975
3. Bonhams sale catalogue, 4 October 1975, p.1
4. Reports appeared in *Women's Wear Daily* (21 July 1975), *Financial Times* (19 July 1975) and *Drapers' Record* (20 September 1975), among other publications.
5. 'Biba's Rude Awakening', *Observer*, 20 July 1975, p.11
6. Prices taken from 'Beside the Seaside', *Pink* (7 February 1974), p.10; 'The Blouses that give shirts short shrift', *Daily Telegraph*, 11 February 1974; and 'Travelling Snugs', *Fabulous* (2 February 1974)
7. 'The day Mrs Biba left a dream world behind', *Evening News*, 12 September 1975
8. Interview with Lilly Anderson, 2 October 2013
9. 'Biba's Barbara gets back to business from Brazil', *The Sunday Telegraph Magazine*, 2 November 1980
10. Ibid.
11. 'Return of a fashion legend', *New Standard*, 10 November 1980, p.9
12. 'Barbara (ex-Biba) bounces back', *The Sunday Times*, 9 November 1980, p.24
13. 'A new shop, a new name, a new look...', *Daily Telegraph*, 10 November 1980, p.17
14. 'Body Clothes', *Cosmopolitan* (November 1980), pp.123–9
15. *Sunday Times Magazine* (9 November 1980), p.100
16. 'Biba goes back to the drawing board', *The Daily Telegraph*, 19 June 1985, p.11
17. 'Body Clothes' (cited note 14)
18. 'Elle Sells', *Elle* (January 1986), p.132
19. Correspondence with Chris Blackwell, 29 July 2012
20. *Independent*, 20 January 1997, p.16
21. Stephen Fitz-Simon, *Being the Boss* (London 1987), p.112
22. 'Topshop's Hulanicki Touch', *Vogue News*, www.vogue.co.uk; accessed 21 April 2009

Further Reading

Michael Bracewell, *Re-make/Re-model. Art, Pop, Fashion and the Making of Roxy Music, 1953–1972* (London 2007)

Christopher Breward, Edwina Ehrman and Caroline Evans, *The London Look: Fashion from Street to Catwalk* (London 2004)

Christopher Breward, David Gilbert and Jenny Lister (eds), *Swinging Sixties: Fashion in London and beyond 1955–1970* (London 2006)

Max Décharné, *King's Road: The Rise and Fall of the Hippest Street in the World* (London 2005)

Nicholas Drake, *The Sixties: A Decade in Vogue* (London 1988)

Peter Everett, *You'll Never be Sixteen Again* (London 1986)

Charlotte Fiell and Emmanuelle Dirix (eds), *Fashion Sourcebook, 1920s* (London 2011)

Elizabeth E. Guffey, *Retro: The Culture of Revival* (London 2006)

Nancy Hall-Duncan, *The History of Fashion Photography* (New York 1979)

Jennifer Harris, Sarah Hyde and Greg Smith, *1966 and All That: Design and the Consumer in Britain 1960–1969* (London 1986)

Catherine Haywood and Bill Dunn, *Man About Town: The Changing Image of the Modern Male* (London 2001)

Bevis Hillier, *The Style of the Century: 1900–1980* (London 1990)

Delisia Howard, *In Biba: A Graphic Romance* (London 2004)

Georgina Howell, *In Vogue: Six Decades of Fashion* (London 1977)

Barbara Hulanicki, *From A to BIBA: The Autobiography of Barbara Hulanicki* (London 2007)

Richard Lester, *Boutique London, A History: King's Road to Carnaby Street* (Woodbridge 2010)

Richard Lester, *Photographing Fashion: British Style in the Sixties* (Woodbridge 2009)

Ruth Lynam (ed.), *Paris Fashion: The Great Designers and Their Creations* (Harmondsworth 1972)

George Melly, *Revolt into Style: The Pop Arts in Britain* (London 1972)

Rainer Metzger, *London in the Sixties* (London 2012)

Eric Musgrave, *Sharp Suits* (London 2009)

Steven Thomas and Alwyn W. Turner, *Welcome to Big Biba: Inside the Most Beautiful Store in the World* (Woodbridge 2006)

Alwyn W. Turner, *The Biba Experience* (Woodbridge 2004)

Judith Watt, *Ossie Clark 1965/74* (London 2003)

Iain R. Webb, *Bill Gibb: Fashion and Fantasy* (London 2008)

Iain R. Webb, *Foale and Tuffin: The Sixties. A Decade in Fashion* (Woodbridge 2009)

Nigel Whiteley, *Pop Design: Modernism to Mod* (London 1987)

Claire Wilcox, *Vivienne Westwood* (London 2004)

Collections

The following collections are represented in the garment pages of this book:

Collection of Murray Blewett pp.108r, 109, 111l, 148, 149r, 152r, 153l, 155r, 194l, 194r, 198r, 203, 206, 207l, 209l

Collection of Brenda Cowood p.153r

Collection of Barbara Hulanicki pp.154, 197r, 201

Collection of Jackie Jackson-Smith p.157

Collection of Irena Michalowska p.207r

Collection of Lady Neale pp.202, 204, 205

Collection of Vivian Parsons p.118

Collection of Mary Peevers pp.159r, 200r

Collection of Sarah Plunkett pp.62l, 63, 65l, 65r, 66, 67l, 67r, 111r, 113, 116l, 116r

Collection of Rosemary Purdy pp.193r, 196

Collection of Jay Read p.197l

Collection of Royal Pavilion & Museums, Brighton & Hove pp.60, 61l, 61r, 62r, 64, 112l, 112r, 115, 119l, 119r, 155l, 192, 193l, 195, 198l, 200l, 208, 209r, 232, 233l, 233r, 235l, 235r, 236, 237, 238, 239l, 239r

Collection of Angie Smith pp.108l, 114, 117, 120, 121r, 150, 151, 156l, 156r, 158, 159l, 199

Victoria and Albert Museum pp.138, 145, 160, 161

Biba Archives at the V&A

Two groups of papers from Biba are preserved in the V&A's Archive of Art and Design, and are accessible in the Museum's archive study room at Blythe House, London.

The firm's press cutting albums, covering the years 1973–5, provide an incomparable record of its impact on British cultural life during the years of 'Big Biba' (ref. AAD/2014/1). The Biba design archives, from the firm of Whitmore-Thomas Associates, document the interior design, graphics and packaging that Tim Whitmore and Steve Thomas devised for Biba over a

seven-year period (ref. AAD/1996/6). They include hundreds of pieces of artwork relating to the decoration, fittings and graphics of the Kensington High Street and Big Biba stores, together with photographs and a comprehensive collection of packaging, posters and other publicity.

The Archive of Art and Design also holds an archive of Barbara Hulanicki's post-Biba fashion business for the years 1981–6, one of the periods when she was living and working in London (ref. AAD/1988/14).

Photographic Credits

Acknowledgements

There are so many people to thank from the last 50 years, since Biba opened. I would like to start with all those who helped us before the opening of the little shop in Abingdon Road, all the beautiful Biba girls (and some boys) who worked in the shop, and the public who supported us by shopping in the stores or from the catalogues – thank you!

I would also like to thank our manufacturers all over Britain, Spain and Italy, as well as Biba Cosmetics in America; Bergdorf Goodman, New York; Royal Pavilion & Museums, Brighton & Hove; Hennes and Mauritz in Sweden; Fiorucci in Italy, and our supporters in France, Miami and, later, Brazil. Thank you, finally, to Poland for the name 'Biba'.

Many thanks to Martin Pel, Mark Eastment and team at the V&A, and book designer Lizzie Ballantyne, for making this book possible.

BARBARA HULANICKI

This book was written following the 2012 exhibition *Biba and Beyond: Barbara Hulanicki* at the Royal Pavilion & Museums, Brighton & Hove, and I would like to thank Professor Lou Taylor, Amy de la Haye and the staff at Brighton Museum for their support – especially Jody East, Helen Grundy, Fiona Redford and Russell Webb from the exhibitions department, as well as Florence Edwards, Helen Le Fevre, Rachel McCarthy-Yardley, E-J Scott and Caroline Sumner.

Many people associated with the original Biba stores, and with Barbara Hulanicki herself, also contributed to my research, with many individuals kindly agreeing to be interviewed for this book. I am incredibly grateful to Lilly Anderson, Sylvia Ayton, Rosie Bartlett, Chris Blackwell, Alicia Bregman, Valerie Cummings, Jo D'Arcy, Victor Edelstein, Allan Gearing, Felicity Green, Barbara Griggs, Louise Kadan, Alison Lang, Lorraine Harper, Julie Hodgess, Delisia Howard, Annie Lennox, Neil Libbert, Antony Little, John McConnell, Cathy McGowan, Molly Parkin, Jennie Peel, Sarah Plunkett, Chris Price, Aileen Ribeiro, Jill Richter, Madeleine Smith, Steve Thomas and James Wedge.

Many people loaned Biba items for inclusion in both the exhibition and this book and I would especially like to thank Murray Blewett, Lisa Eldridge and Angie Smith, as well as Biba Ashmore, Fred Aylward, Galia Bouhayed, Susan Bouhayed, Barbara Burgess, Brenda Cowood, Janet Eden, Liz Eggleston, Jo Graysmark, Susan Groves, Deborah Grubb, Sue Harknett, Annie Hawker, Margaret Howe, Jackie Jackson-Smith, Kelvin MacDonald, Daphne Mair, Irena Michalowska, David Moxley, Vivian Parsons, Mary Peevers, Julie Pitt, June Price-Isles, Louise Prince, Rosemarie Purdy, Joy Read, Barbara Rickwood, Pamela Thomas, Steve Thomas and Janet Tuffs.

I am also very grateful to all the photographers and agents who have given permission for their work to be used in this book, including John Bishop, Guillaume Fabiani, Ron Falloon, Hans Feurer, William Lansbury, Sarah Moon, June Newton and Tiggy Maconochie, Harry Peccinotti, Donald Silverstein and James Wedge.

I would like to say a special thank you to Likrish Marchese at Barbara Hulanicki Design for her warmth and organizational skill, and Terry Clarke for his love and support.

Finally, many thanks to the V&A, to Mark Eastment for his continual interest in the project, Faye Robson for her editorial expertise, Davina Cheung for her attention to the production of this book, Rachel Daley for picture research, and Lizzie Ballantyne for her beautiful book design.

MARTIN PEL

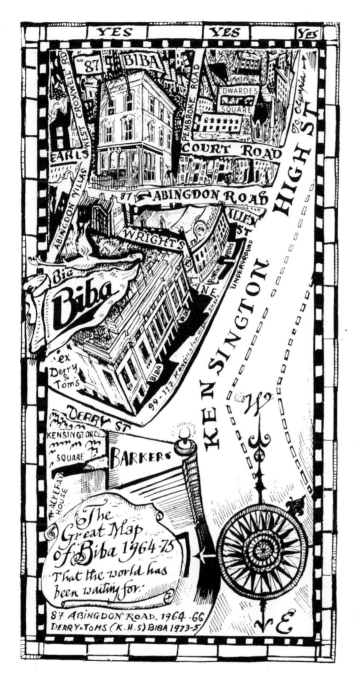

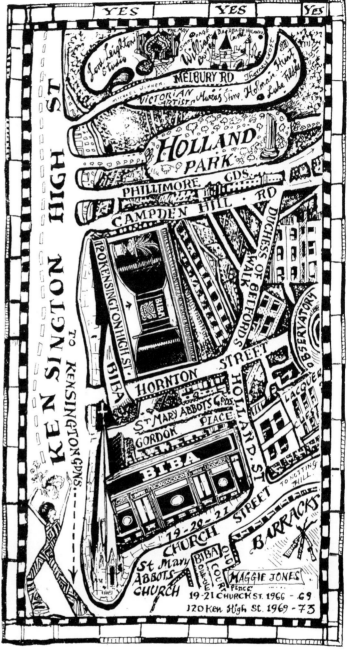

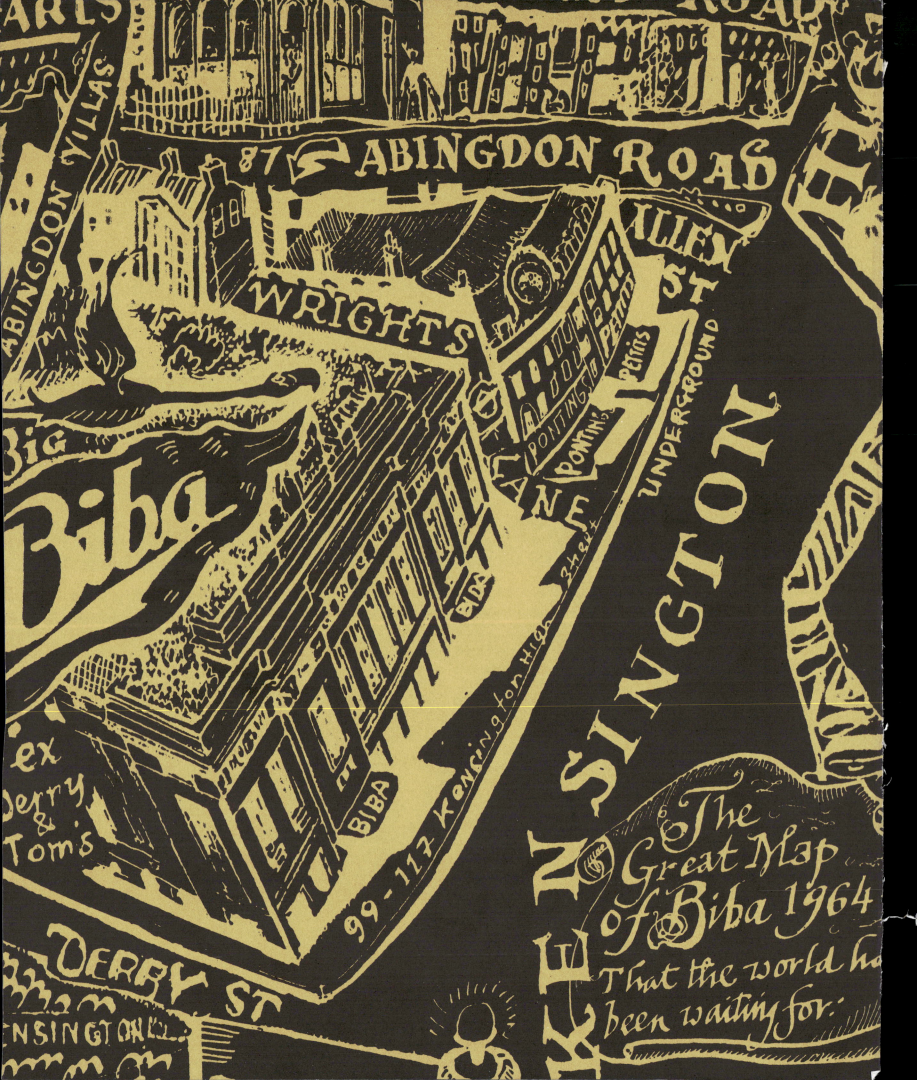